FITTER
FURTHER
FASTER

GET FIT FOR SPORTIVES AND ROAD RIDING

REBECCA CHARLTON, ROBERT HICKS
AND HANNAH REYNOLDS

BLOOMSBURY

LONDON • NEW DELHI • NEW YORK • SYDNEY

Note

While every effort has been made to ensure that the content of this book is as technically accurate and as sound as possible, neither the author nor the publishers can accept responsibility for any injury or loss sustained as a result of the use of this material.

Published by Bloomsbury Publishing Plc
50 Bedford Square
London WC1B 3DP
www.bloomsbury.com

First edition 2013

ISBN (print): 978-1-4088-3261-5
ISBN (ePDF): 978-1-4081-8652-7
ISBN (EPUB): 978-1-4081-8653-4

A CIP catalogue record for this book is available from the British Library.

Acknowledgements
Cover photograph © Roo Fowler,
Inside photographs © Roo Fowler, except the photos of Mark Fenner, Matt Rabin, Mayur Ranchordas and Michael Crebbin (on pp. 134, 74, 84 and 73, respectively), supplied by themselves; and pp. 3 (Doug James), 6 (tswphotography), 17, 79, 85, 143 (Shamleen), 147 (Scott Prokop) and 185 (Doug James) © Shutterstock.com; pp. 14 and 154 © Dan Fleeman; p. 88 © SIS; p. 90 © British Cycling; pp. 97 and 137 © Rapha Condor Sharp; and p. 101 © Team IG-Sigma Sport; illustration on p. 33 by David Gardner
Designed by James Watson
Commissioned by Lisa Thomas

This book is produced using paper that is made from wood grown in managed, sustainable forests. It is natural, renewable and recyclable. The logging and manufacturing processes conform to the environmental regulations of the country of origin.

Typeset in 10pt on 13 MetaPlus by Saxon Graphics Ltd, Derby

Printed and bound in China by C&C Offset Printing Co

10 9 8 7 6 5 4 3 2 1

CONTENTS

Acknowledgements 5
Foreword: Alex Dowsett 7
Introduction... 8

Six months to go 11
   Goal-setting... 12
   Body MOT 16
   Bike fit.. 18
   Clothing and cycling essentials................... 22
   Tools and spares... 25
   Gadgets and gizmos 26
   Gearing 28
   Self-assessment: where are you now? 30
   Nutrition: the basics 32
   Get the legs spinning................................. 38
   Warm-up: is it necessary? 44
   The basics: learn the skills........................ 46
   Cornering: the basics 48
   Climbing: the basics 50
   Descending: the basics.............................. 52
   FAQ... 54

Three months to go 55
   Self-assessment 56
   Aches 60
   Balance and core strength 62
   Balance and core strength exercises............ 64

Pain 70
Refining nutrition 76
Hydration 80
Beyond food: are supplements necessary? .. 83
Beyond food: top ten dietary supplements .. 86
Technical nutrition: gels/powders/bars 88
First aid 92
Crash! 94
Improving skills: cornering 96
Improving skills: climbing 98
Improving skills: descending 100
Taking your fitness to the next level 102
Rest and recovery 110
Burnout 114
FAQ 117

One month to go 119
Self-assessment: are you on track? 120
Quick-fire fitness 122
Refining nutrition 126
Get fit while you work 130
Tapering 132
Nutrition: optimising and maintaining
    weight 136
Pacing 140
FAQ 144

One week to go 145

Self-assessment 146
Don't self-sabotage 148
The importance of TLC 150
Have faith in yourself 152
Carbo-loading 155
Should I race with a cold? 157
Preparing your bike 159

One day to go 161
Night-before nutrition 162
Are you prepared? Is everything ready? 164
Relax! 166
FAQ 167

The big day 169
Morning nutrition 170
Warm-up 173
On the line: what to expect? 175
Stay focused 178
When things go wrong 179

The finish line 181
Warm-down 182
Real rider stories 185
Self-assessment: how did it go? 187
Look to the future, start again 189

Index 191

ACKNOWLEDGEMENTS

We'd like to acknowledge the help of the many coaches, experts and cyclists who provided us with quotes and have shared their experiences with us.

We'd particularly like to thank Alex Dowsett for his patience and humour in answering our many questions and providing us with a foreword. Special thanks also to Stuart Bowers and Symon Lewis for their technical knowledge.

Many thanks to Rupert Fowler for stunning photography and being willing to get on a plane with less than 24 hours' notice. His dedication to lying on tarmac is second to none. Thanks also to Greg Copeland for giving up his time to model and to all the other riders pictured in this book. Special thanks also go to Anne Dickins for helping provide the exercise illustrations, allowing us to use her studio and ensuring the pictures are technically correct. And finally, this project would not have been possible without huge support from Lisa Thomas at Bloomsbury Publishing – it has been such a pleasure working together.

FOREWORD

In cycling, like most other walks of life, the winners and losers are rarely decided on the day. It's about the days, weeks, months and years of training that go into preparing for a single event, whether it's the explosive few seconds that Chris Hoy may sprint in an Olympic final or the three weeks of the Tour de France that Bradley Wiggins suffers both knowing the race can be won or lost in a split second.

Hannah, Rebecca and Rob have been involved, studied closely and written about cycling for a combined total of 30 years. During this time, these writers have amassed an impressive wealth of knowledge that can be applied from grass roots right up to the World Tour level, a range that is difficult to cover. This is coupled with flexibility to their approach that comes with accepting both traditional proven training methods while embracing radical new ideas on extracting the best possible performance from an athlete.

What I love about cycling is how it's all relative. I remember chatting after a local 10-mile time trial one Tuesday evening to a lady who had competed. I had scraped under my 20-minute target while she had completed the course in a more modest time. She commented on a particular section of the course that had been especially gruelling. I emphatically agreed on how tough it was, much to her confusion, 'I'm surprised you even felt that hill the speed you must've been going!' But in cycling, whether at the first rung of the ladder or the top, the sensations of pain and sense of satisfaction upon completing an event are the same.

At Team Sky Procycling we believe there is a thin line between failure and success and this is true for everyone. *Fitter, Further, Faster* aims to give you the knowledge to land on the right side of that line, whatever your goal may be.

I would say good luck, but while we all need a little luck sometimes, I believe that by preparing properly you create your own.

Alex Dowsett,
Professional Cyclist for Team Sky Procycling and
the Great Britain National Team
Essex, March 2012

INTRODUCTION

Cycling is booming and it's not hard to see why so many members of the British public are cottoning onto the benefits of the sport. With a huge and increasing popularity at the professional heights of cycling, after Olympic and world medal success, this is filtering down to amateur level where riders of all abilities can enter a mass participation event or multi-day ride akin to the top level. Sportives are selling out within minutes of hitting the web and the challenges are getting bigger and better, with riders taking on stages of the Tour de France in the Étape du Tour or pushing themselves to the limit on home soil with events like the gruelling three-day Tour of Wessex.

The fantastic element of sportives is that they come in all shapes and sizes so every cyclist can find the right event for them. You may want to start with 10 miles or even 100 miles and whatever your aspirations there will be an event out there for you. The satisfaction of finishing a sportive for the first time, improving on your previous personal best or beating your mates is second to none. Whether you're aiming to make your sportive debut or push further and faster than you have before, this book will take you from start to finish with everything you need to know to not only perform to the best of your ability, but to enjoy the process.

We understand that while you may be aspiring to ride a stage of the Tour, you're not a full-time rider and will have to fit your cycling around other commitments. We appreciate the day-to-day demands and stresses that most of us have as part and parcel of day jobs and life in general. This book will always be on hand for when life gets in the way and, leaving no stone unturned, we'll guide you from the day you fill in that first entry form until you're home and eating your post-event meal.

Fitter, Further, Faster will adapt with you. As you move towards that peak in your performance, whatever your aspiration, your training will change, adapt and evolve. We'll introduce new specifics to work on as you move towards the big goal, including nutrition, hydration, preparation, technique, recovery, core work and all the other elements you need to nail to be at your best. And we'll include top advice and insider tips from top professional athletes, coaches, dieticians and nutritionists.

Starting early is the key to perfect preparation but if you've left it late, don't worry. *Fitter, Further, Faster* focuses on where you are, based on the number of weeks or months you have to go until event day.

Good luck on your sportive journey!

SIX MONTHS
TO GO

SIX MONTHS TO GO

GOAL-SETTING

Before you even think about jumping on a saddle and pedalling off into the distance, stop and ask yourself what it is you want to achieve.

If you want a successful season, and want to avoid riding round in circles slowly going nowhere, then it's imperative to set goals.

Writing down your ambitions on bits of scrap paper may seem a tad dull, but identifying clear outcomes and targets will have a monumental effect on your progression and improvement.

If you don't know what it is you want to achieve, then how on earth are you going to become better? How are you going to become stronger, faster or lighter? Perhaps these aren't your goals at all. But how do you know that if you haven't identified any? You see how confusing it can be. Be smart and make things easy for yourself.

Be SMART

Setting goals is not as easy as you may think. There are many elements to consider, and if you get one of the factors wrong, it could affect your main goal.

Long-term goals are also known as dream goals, and are more often than not looked at as an outcome or as a type of finish line. Now while these are great to have, they won't be achieved unless you set short-term goals, or stepping-stones.

Your goal may be to complete a 100-mile sportive within six months. Great. Now ask yourself what steps you will take to achieve this.

Short-term (for example weekly) or more common daily goals should be your priority. These focus on the present and are far more flexible.

For example, start off on a 10-mile ride, increasing your mileage by 5 miles each week. If you can't get out and ride one day for whatever reason, your short-term goals will allow you to adjust your schedule to make up for the lost days, and you'll know what you have to do in order to meet your weekly goals. You're breaking down your big goal, into smaller, more manageable chunks. A popular method to use when setting goals is the SMART formula. Follow this and you can't go wrong.

Set **Specific** goals. The more specific goals are, the more motivating they will be. For example: 'I want to knock at least 20 minutes off my 50-mile sportive.' This is a precise statement with a finite outcome. You know straight from the start what it is you want to achieve.

Set **Measurable** goals. Many people are too vague when setting goals. I want to become faster. I want to weigh less. This doesn't work. How fast do you want to become? How much weight do you want to lose? You need to able to chart your progress. Losing a specific amount of weight or shaving off a certain amount of time is clear, and documenting your progress along the way will help you clearly identify your progression.

Set **Adjustable** goals. Goals that are set in stone can put too much pressure on you. What happens if you fall sick or incur an injury? You may have to put your training on hold, which could have a huge effect on your target. On the other hand, if a goal is too easy, it may need to be raised. As cyclists we become better pushing barriers.

Set **Realistic** goals. Setting a goal that is unreachable will have absolutely no benefit. Forever pushing yourself in a quest to reach an unobtainable goal will not only leave you exhausted, but also disappointed if the goal hasn't been achieved. Set goals that you can reach, but have to work hard to get there. Easily achievable goals will leave you unfulfilled, and could have a similar deflating effect to that of an impossible goal. Remember, if you follow the SMART principle, you can always adjust them.

Set **Time-based** goals. Breaking your goal down into shorter goals will help keep you focused. For example, you may want to lose one stone by the

Athlete's perspective

Dan Fleeman is a former professional cyclist. In 2008 where he won the Tour des Pyrenees with An Post Sean Kelly. In 2009 Dan rode for the Cervélo Test team, before joining Team Raleigh. He is now director of Forme coaching.

Goals have to be realistic. Determine in advance what the goals you are aiming at will involve. Then start to work back from this objective, and set yourself smaller goals to aim for. This helps keep you motivated and goals in perspective and achievable. This is especially important when things go wrong to keep you focused, for example when injured or sick during training.

time of your next sportive, which is two months away. This may seem a long way away. However, breaking it down into weekly goals – 1.75lb a week – will help you stay more motivated and more likely to stick to it.

How to stick to your goals

Writing down a goal and breaking it into shorter term goals is all well and good, but sticking to them is a whole different matter.

How can we increase the probability of sticking to our goals? Here are five top tips that will help you make sure you stay on track.

1. Don't wait: If you want to ride a sportive this year, then ride a sportive this year. Go and enter it now. Pay the entrance fee. You now have a date set in stone, you've spent your hard-earned cash on it, and you won't run the risk of entries filling up and selling out.

2. Grab a friend: Find someone who you can do it with. This will help with motivation, and will make the planning and riding much more fun.

3. Keep the habit: Habits are formed when they are repeated regularly. You don't have to ride every day, but cycling often enough will keep you hungry for it, and help remind you of what you are working towards.

4. Shout about it: Tell everyone about your goal. Facebook it, tweet it, blog about it. The more people you involve, the more support you'll get, and you'll be less likely to let them down.

5. Be charitable: Ultimately, your goal is for you. However, entering a charity or fundraising ride can give you that extra incentive and keep the motivation strong when you're finding it tough.

then you should take it easy until it is fully cleared up.

2. Are you 100 per cent fit, or are you still sniffling and sneezing from the heavy cold you had a few weeks ago? Once again, wait until it's clear.

Once you have set your goals, and your brand-new bike has arrived, glistening in the hallway, it can be very hard to say no. In fact, it's almost impossible. But you must be sensible. Riding on a pre-existing injury or infection could make things much worse and that '30-minute ride' may set you back further.

The heart of the matter

This is much more serious than searching for aching joints, or runny noses. Do you or have you ever suffered from high blood pressure? Do you have any respiratory problems or suffer from high cholesterol?

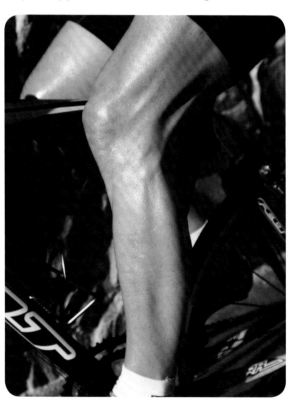

SIX MONTHS TO GO
BODY MOT

Before you start your training period, you must undergo a few preliminary checks. Think of your body as a motorcar. Before you head off on a long journey you'd check the car for any issues or problems. You'd ensure there is enough oil in the engine, the brakes work, the tyres are pumped and that everything is generally in working order. If you do find an issue, you'd get it fixed.

The same exact process can be applied to cycling. Your body is your most important tool, and without it you won't be able turn a pedal.

Make sure you are in the best shape possible before even thinking about getting on the saddle. Cycling has a very good way of uncovering any existing niggles you may have. What's more, it's great at making existing injuries worse and can mean they develop into something far more serious.

Ask yourself these two important questions:

1. Do you have any existing injuries that you are still recovering from? If the answer is yes,

If the answer is yes to any of these questions, go and see a doctor. Ask them whether it's safe to increase your cycling. Be honest with them. Don't tell them that you're riding for a few hours a week when in actual fact you're training for a 100-mile sportive.

Of course, cycling is extremely beneficial to the body and can have huge positives on our fitness. These positives far outweigh the negatives, but there is no denying that the sport puts a lot of pressure on our lungs and our heart.

If you have any problems, then go and get a check-up. Heart screenings may seem a little extreme, but we are now starting to see more and more incidences of athletes in many sports that have run into these types of problems.

If you are worried about these kind of issues and don't know who to see, visit www.cry.org.uk for more information.

Coach's perspective

Huw Williams is a Level 3 BC coach, who has worked with riders all of ages and abilities. He states the importance of health checks.

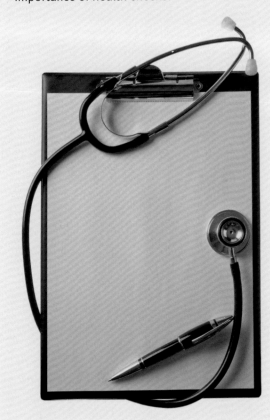

Before starting training be sure you are fit to do so. If there is any history of chronic illness or injury, training will at some point in the near future be at best slightly compromised and at worst a serious health risk. There's not much point in investing a lot of time and money in training and equipment, if at any point you're likely to have to stop due to a pre-existing health condition you could have remedied at the outset. Health screening is a good idea as it can help detect any unknown irregularities in the cardio-vascular system and a physiological assessment of your suitability for your chosen sport is also a good idea. Bike positioning and good core strength are also fundamental considerations. Any muscular imbalance due to incorrect posture on the bike will negatively affect your biomechanics in the highly repetitive pedalling action, while developing good core strength will help your efficiency on the bike, reduce the chance of minor injuries and improve your tolerance to increases in the training load as you improve.

BIKE FIT

Riding a bike for several hours requires both constant repetition of your pedalling motion and holding a rather unnatural posture for an extended period of time. That is what makes the right fit so critical to comfort, performance and injury prevention. At a cadence of 90rpm your legs will turn the cranks 10,800 times in a two-hour ride. That's a lot of opportunities to compound a problem if one exists.

Understanding bike fit

At an elementary level a bike fit can help you make the right decision on frame sizing, but that's really only the first layer of the onion. A bike fit is about the symbiosis of the human body with the bicycle. Only when the riding position on the bike allows the body to function within its optimal ranges of movement can you expect to achieve the best performance with the least chance of injuries and discomfort. It's different for every individual – no one rule necessarily holds true to all – so it's a personal relationship that takes time to develop, it's rarely a 'one-time fix'. When considering your ideal riding position, skeletal and anatomical differences, injury history, flexibility, training loads and participation in other sports all need to be taken into account.

Riding is no fun if you're uncomfortable. This lies at the heart of any good fit; enjoying the simple pleasure of riding means not feeling like you've been beaten up every time you get off your bike. A trained bike-fit technician should be able to help you find the sweet spot between performance, efficiency and comfort.

The good news is, as in so many walks of modern life, technology has come to our aid and cutting-edge techniques have advanced rapidly. What could only be viewed by the human eye 20 years ago can now be studied using digital video, laser sights, and analysed using sophisticated 3-D motion capture software for dynamic fitting. Think of it like old-school car mechanics versus the latest 'plug in' fault-finding telemetry. It's advanced stuff, using the latest fitting jigs changes can even be made and assessed, real time, without the rider even ceasing pedalling.

When to get a bike fit done
At the start: bike fit for a new bike purchase
Bike-fitting can be used as a tool to eliminate guesswork in choosing the right size and geometry to suit your body and riding style. It offers peace of mind that you'll be riding away on the right bike that is set up ready for you to enjoy the experience. This service may be free as part of the sales incentive, but bear in mind some may charge an additional fee. Most retailers will be prepared to swap parts such as stems, bars and saddles as part of the package, to improve or customise fit and perhaps make recommendations for pedals.

As you progress: bike fit for performance increase
It is fairly well accepted that your body has an optimal range of movement, within which it can produce its greatest power and efficiency as well as, importantly, not overstressing certain areas. In a nutshell, poor riding posture could be costing you performance. An advanced bike fit can investigate real-time changes to

SIX MONTHS TO GO

CLOTHING AND CYCLING ESSENTIALS

Having the right kit will make your cycling experience more enjoyable, more comfortable and save you time. The following items are things we consider essential to getting the most from your riding.

Shoes and pedals

We've already mentioned choosing pedals and setting up your cleats correctly in the bike-fitting section, page 21. When buying shoes make sure they have the correct drill pattern on the sole for your cleats to attach to. The sole should be stiff to prevent power loss between your hard-working muscles and the pedals. Look for good ventilation for summer riding as hot feet can become painful on long rides. Try several brands as there can be considerable difference in shape and remember cycling shoes remain stiff, you can't break them

Road shoe or walking shoe?

A road shoe has a completely smooth sole and is designed for optimal power transfer and aerodynamics. They work great on the bike and we recommend them for those serious about racing or target times, however they are not suitable for walking in. A mountain-bike-style shoe with recessed cleats allows you to walk without slipping or damaging the cleat. This may be a better choice for regular commuting or more casual riding.

in, so only buy the ones that feel instantly comfortable.

Cycling socks

Thin, merino or Coolmax socks will help wick sweat away and not be bulky inside your shoe, reducing the risk of pressure points. Height is a fashion issue but somewhere between ankles and mid-calf is generally preferred.

Shorts

Shorts are not something to skimp on, as comfort in the saddle is a key part of enjoying your ride and performing to your best. We recommend bib shorts over waist shorts as they ease the pressure on your belly and give you a smoother profile. As well as being cut differently, the padded insert in men and women's shorts differ in shape with more or less density of padding in certain places. Check the chamois is one-piece with no raised areas of stitching which could cause irritation.

When you try shorts on, get into a riding position because when standing the bibs may cut in or the legs feel too short, which can be misleading. Feel inside the leg grippers to check they aren't too tight.

Look at the cut of the short: the more shape they have the less likely they are to bunch up or twist. Remember: cycling shorts are designed to be worn directly next to the skin.

Base layer

A base layer is worn directly against the skin, its purpose is to wick sweat away from your skin keeping you dry and warm in winter or cool and dry in summer. They need to fit tightly to ensure they don't rub while riding. Ideally you need multiple base layers for different conditions.

Sports bra

The leaning forward cycling position means that gravity is going to have an effect on your boobs. A sports bra will help reduce the pull on skin and ligaments around your chest and can ease shoulder pain if you happen to be very well endowed.

Gloves

Gloves aren't necessarily for keeping hands warm but to protect your palms from the rubbing and pressure of holding the handlebars. If you do crash then gloves will protect your palms from a very painful gravel rash.

Jersey

Cycling jerseys have a few unique features. The cut is shorter at the front, longer at the back and with a high collar so that it is comfortable when in a riding position. And the rear pockets are there for you to stash your food, phone or spares when riding. As with shorts, when trying on a jersey assume a riding position to check the fit.

Helmet

Though not a legal requirement on UK roads you will need a helmet in order to race or ride sportives. Make sure it fits properly and you correctly adjust the pads and straps before leaving the shop. Top-end helmets are lightweight and well ventilated, you will barely know you are wearing one.

Glasses

Glasses are essential kit all year round to keep bugs, grit and rain out of your eyes. Ideally you need a clear and a dark lens option. Choose a reputable brand and always check they have a five-star UVA/UVB rating.

Winter kit
Tights

Thermal Roubaix overtights will keep your legs warm and provide an extra layer on your torso. These can be bought with or without a chamois. In extremely cold conditions choose tights with Windstopper panels on the thighs and shins.

Over shoes

Covering over your shoes helps keep your feet warm and dry and your shoes from getting dirty or damaged. Neoprene is good for wet and cold weather or a Windstopper material for dry, cold days.

Winter gloves

Hands and feet tend to suffer badly on a bike when it is cold. They barely move so there is little blood flow plus they are catching the cold wind as you cycle. If you suffer with cold hands consider using a liner glove and a slightly roomier outer glove as this gives your fingers space to wiggle.

Spring and autumn kit
Knee and arm warmers

Knee and arm warmers are tubes of Roubaix Lycra that can be easily slipped on and off to extend your shorts into tights or provide sleeves for your jersey. They are absolutely indispensable for days, which start off, or end cool as they can be carried in your pockets and put on as needed. They are also great for warming up in, pre-event.

Gilet

A gilet keeps the wind off your torso and provides and extra layer of warmth where you need it. It's a good intermediate on rides when it is too cool for just a jersey but not cold enough for a jacket. A thin Windstopper gilet can easily be carried with you and slipped on if you stop to prevent cooling down.

Chamois cream

Antibacterial and antifungal chamois cream rubbed into your backside and shorts can protect you against saddle sores, friction and discomfort. It's well worth keeping a tub in the bathroom cabinet.

Rollers or turbo trainer

It isn't always sunny outside and sometimes life is too hectic to get a ride in. Static trainers enable you to have a quick time-efficient training session regardless of what else is going on. For structured sessions they can also help you to focus more specifically on the hard efforts you need to be making.

Thermal jacket

A winter jacket may be a significant financial investment but it will enable you to ride all year round and feel toasty warm on even the coldest days. You only need one winter jacket – layering different base layers underneath will help you adapt to different temperatures. Look for Windstopper materials to keep the cold breeze out.

Waterproof shell

Few, if any, jackets will keep you completely dry so focus instead on staying warm on wet rides. If a jacket isn't breathable you may find yourself wetter from your own sweat rather than from the rain and it's just as uncomfortable. A thin shell over a jacket or jersey is often a better choice than an expensive waterproof and it will be small enough to keep in your pocket just in case.

your hands are cold, tyre levers can make the job quicker and easier.

Gas inflator

Compressed gas canisters inflate your tyres to full pressure in a matter of seconds. This is incredibly useful if you want to minimise time loss in an event. Practise using these to inflate your tyres a few times because it can be tricky. Be aware that the canisters get very cold as they expel the gas so never handle them with you bare hands as they will burn you.

At home essentials
Track pump

Mini pumps are useful out on the road but it can be a struggle to get very high pressures into your tyres with them. A floor standing pump will enable you to check tyre pressure frequently and keep your tyres suitably hard. Road tyres should be inflated to between 90–110psi depending on your weight and weather conditions.

Ball-ended Allen keys

While a multi-tool will have a full complement of Allen keys the size of the tool can make simple jobs trickier than they need to be. Full length, ball-ended Allen keys will make simple maintenance jobs much easier to perform.

Torque wrench and Torx keys

Many manufacturers are now using Torx bolts instead of Allen bolts to reduce the chance of rounding out of the bolt head. This is not to be confused with torque settings that are used to prevent over-tightening. A torque wrench that can be set to the manufacturers recommended tightening force will prevent you accidentally damaging components if you have a tendency toward being heavy-handed.

SIX MONTHS TO GO

TOOLS AND SPARES

On the road essentials
Spare tubes

Punctures are an inevitable part of cycling. Carry a minimum of two tubes at all times so that when you get a flat you can quickly change a tube instead of fiddling around with a puncture repair kit.

Multi-tool

A multi-tool should have everything you need to make any roadside repairs including a chain splitter. A snapped chain is impossible to fix without a chain tool so learning how to use it and carrying one can save a lot of inconvenience if it does happen to you.

Pump

A lightweight mini-pump will be able to get enough pressure into your tyres for you to complete your ride safely.

Tyre levers

With practice you should be able to change a tyre without using levers but for stiff tyres, or days when

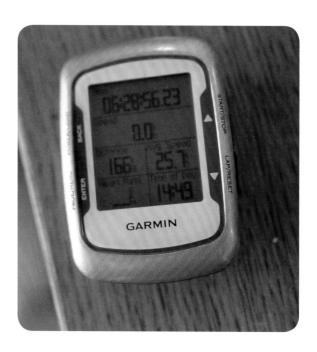

GADGETS AND GIZMOS

When you're aiming for a big event on the bike it's easy to feel bombarded with fancy high-tech gadgets that you could potentially buy. Not only could this become a very expensive habit but recording every element of data can potentially distract you from the task at hand and reduce your enjoyment of simply being on your bike. Differentiating between useful tools for your development and nice-to-haves will help to avoid technology overload when you're working towards your event goal.

One of the first things to remember is that you are unique, so when it comes to looking at data you should simply mark your progress and avoid comparing your numbers to other people's. It can be fun to use online software to see how you measure up to your mates but do not get disheartened if they are in a different place in their training to you.

There is absolutely nothing wrong with training on how your body feels and measuring your improve-ments by keeping up with mates or commuting home that bit faster, for example. However, if you want to give yourself a helping hand, a heart-rate monitor (HRM) will allow you to determine your resting heart rate, as well as your maximum threshold. HRMs can be extremely useful in targeted training sessions where you aim to hit various zones of intensity, based upon your max. See pages 41–42 for more information on training zones.

Various speed, cadence and power computers can also be attached to the bike in order to both measure progress and target training sessions. Measuring speed can be very useful in determining the time you're aiming to do on event day and how you need to train to achieve that. Aiming to increase the averages over the duration of your rides, as well as increasing the distance gradually, will be easier with a speed computer. Power is where things become slightly more complicated and is perhaps a gadget to be introduced later should you feel you want to further analyse your training.

Athlete's perspective

Alex Dowsett began his professional cycling career with the Great Britain Olympic Academy, moving to Trek-Livestrong to ride with Lance Armstrong and now resides with Team Sky.

Where this young rider has really made his mark is on the time-trial circuit where pacing and schedules are absolutely crucial to clock up the best time on the day. Similarly, when you're riding a sportive, going out too fast will affect your legs in the later stages of the ride so it's important to understand how far you can push yourself while saving some gas for later. But how much is this down to feel and how much should you rely on numbers and data? Alex tells us how it works at the elite level and whether it's necessary for riders of all standards.

"It's very important for my coaches to look at data. We use training peaks software so pretty much every pedal stroke can be downloaded and analysed. Obviously, this isn't always the case and I train a lot on feel but when it's time to look at numbers my coach can see exactly where I'm at and adjust training and training zones accordingly. It's also handy to see progression throughout my career as well as I become older and stronger.

In terms of training on feel, it's very important to listen to your body. I often train using a three-days-on/one-day-off approach but if the three days is harder than planned then sometimes it's necessary to take two easy days. Rest is far more important than training in a lot of cases, I know if I spend the day on my feet I wont feel great next day on the bike. My coach often either holds me back or pushes me on depending on whether I'm getting carried away or being plain lazy.

I use the new SRM PowerControl 7, which is a godsend for telling me if I'm being lazy in important training sessions.

For riders who can't afford all the latest kit I'd say you don't need it in order to improve; the fancy bikes and kit and training software helps but anyone who is anyone in cycling started out with the basics and worked their way up.

logical. We see a lot of cyclists failing to use the big ring, small ring or 'granny ring' at the front appropriately. Leaving your chain on the big ring at the front and making things lighter at the back by using the largest sprocket isn't ideal as this stretches the chain. Instead, shift down a couple at the back in preparation to drop down to the smaller ring at the front if you're finding the gear too big. This way you avoid spinning away or dropping a chain by shifting too dramatically all in one go.

Clunk and grind

The other element of changing through the gears is to avoid clunking and crunching through the sprockets. You can avoid this by thinking about each change and practising it when you're out on the road. As domestic pro-rider James Millard explains, you need to avoid having all of your pressure on the cranks as you make that shift:

'Always err on the side of caution with gear changes, do it early, smoothly and precisely. No one wants to be labouring in a massive gear and having to panic to change down five gears in one go! Always lift ever so slightly off the power before you change gear as a chain with less pressure on it will change in a much smoother and more predictable fashion, try to do this just before the top of the pedalling stroke so the gear is engaged for the more powerful down stroke.'

SIX MONTHS TO GO

GEARING

Smooth gear changes can make or break a good ride. Not only do you need your gear cables to be in perfect working order but learning how to shift up and down efficiently will make things significantly easier.

It may sound simple: click the lever and the gear changes. However, you'll often see riders crunching and grinding gears, which not only impacts on the life of your chain but also can lead to immediate problems on a ride. Familiarise yourself with the basic gear ratios and you'll find things are pretty

Fitter, Further, Faster top tips

- Take the pressure off the pedals when changing gear
- Look ahead and plan your gear changes until it becomes second nature
- If things become noisy, take a look at the gear combination
- If you keep dropping your chain, get your cables checked out
- If the chain is skipping sprockets your gears may need adjusting
- If in doubt, get to a local bike shop
- Avoid making massive changes in one go
- Don't be lazy and stick it in the big ring all day, spinning is good!

Ups and downs

Thinking ahead to what's approaching is key to the efficient use of your gears. If you know you're on a rolling stretch of road, keeping up your momentum can give you a real performance gain and this is where planning your gears comes in. If you push over the crest of a hill straight onto a descent you want to get into a gear quickly and smoothly which allows you to pedal on the downwards slope. Similarly, look up the road ahead, and if there's another hill approaching, get ready to shift into the appropriate gear to retain that momentum, but without leaving yourself pushing the biggest gear and grinding to a halt. You may find it's better to click down on the rear sprockets towards the end of the descent in order to drop to the smaller ring at the front just before you hit the incline. Practice makes perfect!

Cables

If, when you first got your bike, things were running smoothly but now you're constantly dropping your chain or your gears skip of their own accord you will need to check your cables or pop to your local bike shop for a service. Cables will need replacing from time to time as they can stretch or become worn and tired and this will affect your gear changes.

SELF-ASSESSMENT
WHERE ARE YOU NOW?

You've looked into events, targeted your goals for the season and now you probably want to plunge straight into hard training. However, this is the perfect time to assess where you are right now in order to measure your progress as you go forward. Work out realistically how many hours you can devote to your training because training without structure can leave you unsure of your physical development or could even lead to illness due to putting too much pressure on your body. Jot down where you feel you're at – for example, 'I'd like to lose half a stone' or 'I need to work on my climbing'. It's also important to run a field test in order to tangibly track your progression. We'll be suggesting you repeat the self-assessment process in three months' time so this will offer a motivational starting point and you can compare the numbers down the line.

Resting heart rate
We mentioned in 'Gadgets and gizmos' (pages 26–27) that a heart-rate monitor can be a good personal indicator of where your body is at. Now is the perfect time to take your resting heart rate over the duration of a week. You will need to observe the readings for longer than a day or two to establish an average and real figure for this as your reading can change due to many factors such as caffeine consumption, over-tiredness or illness. The best time to take this measurement is first thing in the morning when you are lying down and at complete rest. Once you have gathered what you feel is your true resting figure, make a note of it in your training diary and watch what happens in line with training over the next few months. You should expect to see a drop if you are making large fitness gains.

Coach's perspective

John Scripps is a talent development coach for British Cycling so has plenty of experience in measuring the progress of his riders across the country. Here he describes a simple way to start your self-assessment.

To measure your improvements and in order to progress, go out and set a field test. Try to find a climb that you can go out and repeat, practise on and then it's a case of using that climb to build power. You can simply time yourself from the start to the finish of the climb, and as you get stronger through the climbs, in theory you should get quicker. Obviously there are factors that will affect your time, for example, whether it's wet, whether it's windy, cold or warm and what kit you've got on. If it's cold you're going to be wearing more kit and carrying more weight with you. If you're on a longer ride you might have more kit in your pockets so if you're going to do a field test, try to keep all the variables as similar as you can, i.e. wear similar kit, on the same bike and bear in mind the gearing you're doing to testing on as well.

The same rule can apply for a climb near you or a 10-mile out and back stretch of road from your house. Time yourself and write it down. Also note, how you feel about certain elements of your chosen test, for example, do you find the hill tough? Do you look forward to the descents or do they cause you concern and in general, how happy are you with your technical skills?

Check your vital stats

In addition to your heart rate, now is the time to take note of the numbers relating to your body composition. Weigh yourself and, if possible, check your body fat percentage via electronic scales or a calliper test. Don't forget to get a good old-fashioned measuring tape and take your waist, leg and chest measurements.

NUTRITION
THE BASICS

Eating well is fundamental for your physical health and well-being but eating should also be an enjoyable experience. If you enjoy your food and pay attention to what you eat you will likely have a healthier diet and more energy for your cycling.

Make a start

There are all manner of products and diets aimed at sports people, and it's easy to get suckered in to thinking you need the latest supplement, new energy drink or fancy diet plan – but most are completely unnecessary. Eating healthily should be a long-term part of your lifestyle so we aren't going to push any kind of restrictive diet or quick-fix weight-loss plan. Instead, we are going to offer you some simple changes that will allow you to clean up your existing diet so that you feel better and have more energy for your cycling. If you are keen to lose weight then a well-balanced diet and increase in regular exercise will help set you on the path to that goal as well.

What makes a healthy diet?

Let's start with the foods that should make up your daily diet. The Food Guide Pyramid (see page 33) is widely recognised as being the basis for healthy eating. The emphasis is on the importance of grains, fruits and vegetables. Unrefined carbohydrates such as wholemeal bread and pasta, wholegrain cereals and rice, lentils and beans should make up half to two thirds of your calorie needs. The next layer up is the protective and nutrient-rich fruits and vegetables, ideally you should be eating two to four servings of fruit per day and three to four servings of raw or lightly cooked vegetables.

In the third tier up you'll find your primary protein sources such as meat, poultry, fish, eggs, beans, nuts and dairy. These should make up a quarter of your daily foods. The final pinnacle is a very small amount of sweets, fats and sugars, which offer very small amounts of fibre or nutrients and in some cases may even be counterproductive to good

health as they are linked to health problems such as obesity, heart disease and cancer. Eat these as an occasional treat.

How to start cleaning up your diet

One of the biggest barriers to eating healthily is time and organisation. If you are in a rush it is much easier to grab a ready-made sandwich or hit the vending machine at work. When you get home of an evening, if there is nothing in the cupboard you are more likely to snack on quick, easy but less nutritious foods such as an oven pizza or take-away. There is nothing wrong with this occasionally, we all know that feeling when we can't be bothered to cook, but the reality is you will wake up the next morning with less energy. You may also find that you've put on a bit of weight and you may suffer more colds because you aren't eating the nutrients you need to boost your immune system. If you want to progress as a bike rider the healthier your diet is, the better you will feel and the more energy you will bring to your training sessions.

So, stage one of improving your diet is taking stock of what is in your cupboards at home and turfing out the foods that are likely to sabotage your new clean way of eating. Get rid of those packets of crisps, sugary breakfast cereals or biscuits that you are likely to grab when you are peckish. Don't rely on your willpower to resist, get them out the house altogether. If they aren't there you can't eat them.

You may now find yourself surveying empty shelves but don't worry about that yet. The second stage is to take stock of your own cooking and food-preparation abilities. The healthiest meals are what you prepare yourself from whole foods. This way you are in control of the quality of the ingredients, the portion sizes and the addition of other things such as salt and fat. There are plenty of simple meals you can quickly throw together yourself even with very few cooking skills. However this might be a good point at which to invest in a few recipe books. Avoid any of the 'diet' titles, go for something that features foods you like and looks easy to follow.

Shopping

The most efficient way to shop is to plan your menu for the week and buy only the ingredients you need. This prevents food wastage and means you have everything you need to make cooking as simple and quick as possible. Another way to do it is to carry the idea of the food pyramid over to your supermarket experience.

Start in the fresh fruit and veg aisle, make sure your trolley is half full of colourful fruits and vegetables, as they will take up the largest volume of all your meals and snacks. Head for the aisle with fresh meats and fish, opt for one red meat, a couple of poultry and at least two oily fish meals. In the diary aisle, as well as milk grab a small amount of cheese and low-fat yoghurts for snacks and desserts. Skip the crisps and biscuits aisle entirely. Choose some wholemeal pasta, rice, quinoa and cous cous, plus healthy cereal choices such as porridge or muesli. If you aren't confident in cooking sauces look for ready-made tomato-based sauces with a limited amount of added sugar, salt and fat.

Easy swaps

Food	*Swap for*
White bread	✓ Brown bread
Juice	✓ Whole fruits
Crisps	✓ Dried fruit and nuts
Ready meals	✓ Home-cooked meals
Salt	✓ Herbs and spices

Knowing your portion sizes

Cleaning up your diet and swapping some of your treat food for healthier snacks will go a long way to helping change your waistline. Eating higher volumes of fruit and veg, and swapping white for wholemeal, will help you feel full up because of their high fibre content so even without deliberately cutting back you will naturally eat fewer calories. Another thing to look at if you are trying to get a grip on your diet is portion size.

Eating healthily should not feel difficult. The simpler you make it the more likely you are to stick to a clean healthy diet. Instead of measuring out your food, try following these simple guidelines to make sure you are eating the right portion size for you at every main meal.

- **PROTEIN**
(meat, fish, poultry, nuts, eggs) 1 serving per meal.

Your protein portion should be the same size as the palm of your hand.

- **CARBOHYDRATE**
(wholegrain cereals, rice, pasta, potatoes) 1 serving per meal.

Your carbohydrate serving should be the same size as your clenched fist.

- **FRUIT AND VEGETABLES**
2–3 different types per meal.

Your fruit and vegetable serving should fill to overflowing two cupped hands.

Nutritionist's perspective

If you want to make healthy eating a permanent fixture you need to make it part of your routine. Commit to a weekly shop to stock your cupboards with healthy options and experiment with recipes to avoid boredom. If it's difficult to stick to healthy eating at work, brown bag your lunch and keep healthy snacks at your desk. By doing so you won't leave yourself with any excuse for straying from your healthy diet.

Laura Tilt Nutritionist (MSc),
Dietician (PG Dip)

SIX MONTHS TO GO

GET THE LEGS SPINNING

Everyone wants to get fit or fitter but the question you must ask yourself is 'fit for what?' Before you start planning your sessions or prepare to commit to a training plan your first task is to take a good look at your target event and work out its demands. What distance is it? How long do you think it will take you to finish? Is it hilly? Are there long steady alpine climbs or short, steep British ones? Will you be riding alone or in a bunch? Will your bike handling skills make a difference? Will there be long fast descents?

Once you've got the answers to these questions you can start to look at your own strengths and weaknesses. If it is a long ride, do you already have good endurance or will the biggest challenge be managing the distance? If it is hilly how easy do you find climbing? Maybe this is an area you need to work on. How experienced are you at riding with others? Should you do a shorter, easier event first so you can

practise? An hour or so looking at the course details, sifting through forums for other riders' experiences of the event and having a good look at your own fitness and experience will be time well spent.

Lifestyle audit

When you take up a new sport or fix your sights on an exciting challenge it is very easy to over-commit yourself. Now is the time to be realistic about how much time you can dedicate to improving your cycling. Suddenly finding a spare five hours or more in your already busy week can be a challenge. Professional coaches audit their athletes' lifestyles before setting a training plan so as you are your own coach you need to do this for yourself. Keep a diary for a week and fill in what you are doing during every hour of the day. Be honest. At the end of the week you will see how much cycling time you already have and areas where you could carve out a little more. If you want more time to ride can you get up a little earlier? Forgo some of your usual sofa or TV time? Could you cycle to work some days? We look more at this on pages 130–131.

Where are you now?

Building fitness needs to be controlled and progressive; pile on too much too soon and you may find yourself ill, injured or excessively tired. Often when riders start a plan they think it is way too easy, but in fact this is how it should be. If it feels hard in the first few weeks you almost certainly won't stick with it as it begins to increase in effort. How much riding are you currently doing a week? This is your starting point, the first month you won't need to do much more than you already are. If you are starting from zero then the first few weeks will be less than five hours, just 30 minutes to an hour for each ride. For more on self-assessment flick back to pages 30–31.

Planning your route

This book's format is designed around the journey of starting preparation for a goal event: training for it, eating for it, riding it and recovering from it. An ideal time frame from entering an event to doing it is three to six months, as this gives plenty of time to improve your fitness while remaining a manageable chunk of time to stay focused on one goal.

Between now and your goal event we need to manage your fitness progress by balancing training efforts with recovery. When you exercise it provides a stress upon your body; for a short while after a block of training your performance appears to drop as your body is tired. Given the right amount of rest your body learns to cope with the stress put on it and becomes stronger than it was before.

If you then stop exercising, your fitness level begins to drop again so you need to add more stress or a different kind of stress, and again your body adapts to deal with it and yet again becomes stronger. See pages 110–111 for more information on the effect of exercise on the body.

Understanding training zones

On pages 26 and 27 we looked at various gadgets and gizmos, such as heart-rate monitors and power meters that enable you to measure your effort levels when you are cycling. Working at different effort levels stress your body in different ways, the type of stress determines what areas of your fitness will improve, how hard the session feels and how long it will take you to recover from it. Below is a table explaining what the training zones are called, how it feels to ride at that effort level and what purpose it serves in improving your fitness. These training zones are widely used and are the zones recognised by British Cycling coaches. We've also provided other commonly used terms that you may have read elsewhere to help avoid confusion.

Understanding zones

Zone	Also known as	Feels like	Purpose
Zone 1	Very easy Recovery pace	Easy, you can talk comfortably in full sentences and it requires little concentration. You could ride like this all day if you needed to.	Zone 1 rides are normally for recovery after harder training and the start and end of rides as a warm-up or warm-down. This ride puts very little stress on your body but spinning your legs gently can help flush out your muscles and relax you.
Zone 2	Easy	You will need to start concentrating on your riding but it is only a small amount of focus just to stop you drifting back to a too easy pace or picking it up to a slightly harder pace. You will still be able to talk in short sentences.	Zone 2 rides are for building endurance. Developing how your body uses fat as a fuel and for getting you used to sitting on the bike for extended periods of time. When you first start cycling a lot of your time will be at this zone to help build up your fitness.
Zone 3	Hard-steady	This is a reasonably hard effort, you will still be able to talk in brief sentences but need to pause for breath more often. Breathing will still be regular and not ragged but will be deeper and more frequent.	Working at this zone improves your body's ability to extract oxygen from the air and transport it to your muscles, using fat as a fuel for exercise. This is a pace that you would be able to complete a long sportive at.
Zone 4	Brisk Fast-steady Sweet spot tempo Aerobic threshold	This requires concentration and is best done on your own. Conversation is no longer possible as you will be breathing deeply and frequently. It is hard but manageable, you should be able to sustain this effort for 10–20 minutes.	Zone 4 is based around your aerobic threshold, it helps increase the power you can produce aerobically but is also pushing up your lactate threshold, so improving the power you can produce before you tip over the red line where the lactic-acid burn begins.
Zone 5	Anaerobic threshold	Zone 5 is the thin red line between hard yet comfortable and thigh burningly tough. It is your maximum sustainable pace, you could do a 20–30 minute race at this pace but no more. It requires a significant amount of concentration to maintain.	At Zone 5 your muscles are producing and disposing of lactic acid so work at this zone improves your body's ability to remove lactic acid whilst maintaining a significantly high pace. Work at this zone raises the maximum pace you can sustain over an extended period of time.
Zone 6	Very hard Interval training	You cannot sustain this effort for more than 3 minutes at a time. It is very hard and requires you to be able to push yourself despite discomfort.	Intervals vary in length from the 10–15 second efforts to 3 minutes maximum. Recovery between efforts needs to be of equal length or longer. Work in this area develops bursts of very high speed or power for short hill climbs, sprints and attacks in a race.

Three key rides

This stage of your preparation is often referred to as 'base building'. Your goals are to develop your endurance and the amount of time you can comfortably ride for, develop your cycling skills and strengthen your cycling-related muscles. Aim to do between three and five rides per week, making sure you always have at least two days when you don't ride at all. Try and build the length of continuous riding you do on your long rides. Start with an hour without stopping and build by no more than 15 minutes every week. It may not sound like much of an increase but over the next three months that will take your one-hour ride up to four hours in steps so small you will never feel out of your comfort zone.

1. *The long ride*

Frequency: 1–2 times every 7 days
Intensity: Zone 1 and 2
Duration: 60 minutes–4 hours
Progression: Add 15 minutes to your long ride every week, no more than that. Keep it to Zone 2 for the majority of the ride although you may tip into Zone 3 on some of the longer hills.

2. *Cadence drills*

Frequency: 1–2 times every 7 days
Intensity: Zone 1 and 2
Duration: 30–60 minutes
Progression: Mix up these different drills to develop the smooth pedalling stroke and efficient cadence all bike riders need. Ideally you would do this on the turbo, if you do it on the road make sure it is safe, traffic free and flattish.

3. *Technique*

Frequency: 1–2 times every 7 days
Intensity: Zone 1 and 2
Duration: 30–60 minutes
Progression: Improve your speed and confidence by varying your route and introducing new challenges. Over the next three months you should become comfortable riding on the drops for corners and descents.

Using the advice on pages 46–53 plan routes that include left-hand corners (so you don't need to stop), short climbs and descents to practise your bike position and handling skills.

Cadence drills

One-legged pedalling

Unclip one foot and let it hang or hold it behind you. Pedal for one minute using one leg at around 50rpm concentrating on maintaining a smooth circle. Listen out for any clonking from your free-wheel that shows you aren't maintaining an even pressure. Clip both feet back in and pedal at 90rpm for a minute then unclip the other leg. Repeat for 15 minutes until you have done 5 minutes on each leg.

Spin-ups

Change into a very easy gear and gradually wind up your pedalling over 30 seconds till you are turning your legs as fast as you can without bouncing in the saddle then hold that pace for 30 seconds. Recover for one minute at a slower cadence and repeat. Do one minute fast, one minute slow for ten minutes.

Big-gear circles

Pedal for 5 minutes using a big gear that requires you to pedal at no more than 50rpm. As you are pedalling visualise the circles your feet are turning. Keeping both feet clipped in, focus your mind on one leg at a time to try and feel the sensations in each muscle group as they work.

SIX MONTHS TO GO

WARM-UP

IS IT NECESSARY?

Most of us do warm up, but if you ask us why we do it, not many people really know the answer.

Some people will gently spin their legs to get them warm, others will push hard in order to get their heart beat up and then there are some who do nothing at all.

It's not just the sportive rider who is unsure about the benefits of a proper warm-up. Many athletes find it confusing, with the common misconception that a long warm-up will only serve to tire you out and eat away at your precious energy reserves.

This is not the case – providing you know what to do. A pre-ride warm-up may not only reduce the risk of injuries, but will also help the body switch from a resting state to maximal exercise in preparation for the onset of heavy exercise.

An efficient warm-up will have numerous physiological benefits such as:

- Increase in muscle temperature: a warmed muscle will contract more forcefully and relaxes quicker resulting in an increase in speed and strength.
- Increase in body temperature: muscle elasticity will improve reducing the risk of strains and pulls.
- Increased blood flow.
- Reduction of stiffness: movement becomes greater and resistance lowers when muscles are warm.
- Higher heart rate: heart is prepared for the onset of exercise, and heart rate is being built up gradually.

When to do what?

One reason why there is so much confusion surrounding warm-ups in cycling is due to the vast amount of different disciplines within the sport. For example, a time trial, a track sprint, a road race and a sportive will all require different warm-ups in order to best prepare the body. The fact of the matter is regardless of the type you're doing, even if it's part of your commute to work, then you should partake in a warm-up of sorts.

Warm up your mind as well as your body

A warm-up will also improve your psychological well-being. A good warm-up is a perfect time to mentally prepare yourself for an event. Your concentration will heighten, as you are in an environment similar to that of your event, therefore raising your focus and attention.

Athlete's perspective

Olympic medallist and ex road racer, Rob Hayles shares his views on warm-ups.

"Warm-ups are quite odd, as many people have different views on the subject. I've known some riders who don't warm up and have gone into an event and have flown round. On the other hand, some have warmed up and have struggled. I think sometimes it's more down to luck than judgement in how your body reacts and where you are in your programme.

Personally, I wouldn't overdo a warm-up. Don't go too deep. You have to prepare the body for what it's about to do but without going into your reserves. There have been some cases where people go too deep and their muscles can't recover in time for the event. They end up going harder in the warm-up than the event, which is ridiculous.

Start to realise the importance of a warm-up, and incorporate it into your cycling. For the first 15 minutes of every ride, don't over do it. Spin your legs at good cadence with a little resistance, gradually rising to your normal riding speed. This way, you are breaking your body in for the exercise that is due to be placed upon it, and reducing the shock that is placed on the body when people go from no exercise to full throttle.

If you wish, put the occasional hard ten second efforts in, to raise your heart and respiratory rate, and get the legs firing.

It's important to note that different types of cycling require different warm-ups. A general rule of thumb, the shorter the event the longer the warm-up needs to be. Remember, a warm-up is to prepare the body for an event, not tire it out.

Go to pages 173–174 for a descriptive plan of how best to prepare for a sportive.

SIX MONTHS TO GO

THE BASICS
LEARN THE SKILLS

Nailing the basics will provide you with the perfect foundation to start building up your skill set and, in turn, your overall performance. While you'll be eager to get going with the mileage it's crucial to spend time practising technique, however simple it may seem because this will pay dividends on the day of your event.

A lack of confidence or knowledge of how the bike handles can waste a significant amount of time and energy when you're against the clock. Plenty of riders neglect the basics and this is where you can really make vast improvements. Not only will this chapter help your performance it will also increase your knowledge of good safety, as wise bike handling will help you out of situations that may otherwise result in coming off the bike.

Drafting

In terms of making your life easier and allowing your hard-earned fitness to go further; 'drafting', 'slipstreaming' or 'sitting in' are common expressions, that you need to be familiar with. The closer you can safely get to the wheel in front of you the easier your ride will be because you can save around 30 per cent of your effort by allowing the person in front to take the brunt of the wind and break the air for you. By sitting in that magical void you will reap the benefits.

If you've not drafted before it's a good idea to go somewhere quiet to practise with another rider, for example a remote stretch of road where you're unlikely to meet traffic. Start off at a distance you feel comfortable with and then move closer and closer as you build confidence. In theory, the nearer the better as you'll gain the maximum benefit of the wind protection but that said, there's no point in being that close if you're not confident in the wheel you are following, so avoid overlapping and ensure you have an escape route should you need it. We'd always recommend looking for the largest person in the group if you're struggling to keep the pace because, again, this will save you energy.

Etiquette

Drafting can make all the difference to your legs and time on the day of your event and similarly can significantly affect how you go in training. If you're lucky enough to have a group of local riders you can go out with, you really will be able to go further and faster with a little help from your friends. By working efficiently as a group you'll be surprised by how fast you can drift along without feeling anywhere near as fatigued as you would if you were training alone. However, this can have drawbacks too. Keep an eye on your training zones as riding with others can encourage you to ride too fast or too slow.

Unwritten rules

However, if like many riders you are riding the sportive with an individual target in mind there are some unwritten rules of etiquette that are good to bear in mind so as to pedal harmoniously with others. If you're feeling good it can be tempting to sit in behind a bunch of riders, then hop between groups to get yourself ahead. While this isn't necessarily a problem we'd always advise greeting riders that you come up to, and if you plan to ride with them, let them know, and do your fair share of work! The same goes for training rides and commutes – some riders will be flattered that you're tailing them on the way home from work while others can get rather wound up if there is no camaraderie to accompany it.

it wrong occasionally. If you're not familiar with a rider's style and they hammer into the turn fast it doesn't necessarily mean they have more technical nous than you, and this can lead to things going awry. Rather than jumping in the deep end and trying to focus on speed, it's more important to practise your individual technique at a slower pace, even if it means you get left behind or increases your overall ride time: if you get it wrong you'll more likely end up on the floor rather than getting ahead!

Technique

One of the first rules of cornering is to look at where you want to end up rather than where you don't! If you're concerned about avoiding a bush or overshooting the bend, it can be tempting to avert your gaze to the obstacle – the chances are that if you stare at it you will veer towards the very place you don't want to be. Instead pick your line and look for your exit point with confidence.

If you have a riding mate that you trust, it's great to practise sitting on their wheel and copying what they do. If you're on your own, have a think about approaching a little wider into the corner, so that you can cut in at the tightest part, this is what riders describe as 'hitting the apex'. That way you're essentially smoothing out the line you take, keeping things as straight as possible or in a nice arc. It's important to remember at any level of cornering is

CORNERING
THE BASICS

Your cornering skills can make all the difference when it comes to sportives. Build your confidence in this key riding element and you will see great gains. Experience is significant here and so practice makes perfect. By learning how it feels to lean the bike and pick up speed you will gradually be able to determine how quickly you can safely pull off a tight corner and recognise where and when you need to kill the speed.

The main thing to bear in mind at this stage of your training is that you need to ensure you are confident and happy with your own technique before trying to follow other riders who may have a different level of skill to you. Getting the basics right first will ensure you're as safe as possible and avoid unnecessary spills.

Riding in a group has many benefits, however it's important to get to know the wheels you are following to make sure you trust their judgement, rather than following blindly, because everyone gets that while the professionals race on closed circuits, giving them the luxury of sweeping across the entirety of the course, you must account for traffic and avoid ending up on the wrong side of the road. So while the optimum line is cutting from the outside of the road into the bend, it's not always realistic.

As you start to build your speed you'll need to think about your pedal position to avoid clipping the ground. Scraping your pedal can be disastrous so ensure that you push your outside leg down while leaning through anything tight, then resume pedalling when you return to a more upright position.

Relax

Keeping your body relaxed on the bike is key across all the skill sets but for cornering it can make or break your technique. Panicking and hitting the brakes halfway through a turn is not a good idea as you run the risk of losing control of the bike, so the more you can keep your body and mind calm, the more you will exit a turn happier and more comfortable. You will be able to lean the bike further as you build your training and get a better feel for a range of turns. The more your commit the easier it will become, but there's no need to rush it.

Your braking needs to be done before you hit the bend so that you're entering it at a speed you know you can pull off. If you feel you've gone in too fast, avoid trying to correct it by grabbing at the brakes and instead make every move as smooth as possible. The less you stiffen up, the better and always remember to keep your head up allowing you to look ahead.

CLIMBING
THE BASICS

Many riders dread hills, which means they get a pretty bad press despite being where most people will make the biggest fitness gains. This probably comes down to the fact that climbing is a really individual element of cycling; it can be tough and it can really divide the abilities. Most of us will have experienced that moment when the elastic snaps, you're breathing hard but the guy next to you isn't and it can become disheartening.

Coach's perspective

Here's John Scripps, a talent development coach for British Cycling, on all the ways we can learn to love those lumps and bumps.

Firstly, try and relax through the climb and try to avoid fighting the gradient, because if you spend the whole time fighting the climb you'll waste energy. So stay nice and relaxed and position your body up on the tops. Also sit quite balanced on the bike, so don't put too much weight forward because you could end up losing traction at the back. On the other hand, if the hill is really steep and you're trying to put too much body weight back, that's when your front wheel can lift.

With gearing, try and keep things light as opposed to going for heavy gearings, because if you over gear on a long climb it's going to feel like a long old climb and you'll end up sapping energy that way. So go for high cadence and lower gears, rather than pushing and labouring the big options.

Keep your body still, rather than moving it around so you're just focusing your effort into pushing up the climb rather than swinging your body round.

Pacing

Your strongest part of the effort should be towards the last part of the climb, rather than going out and up as fast as you can and getting really slow when you reach the top. Instead, start off steady and build up with what you've got and when you get to the top, that should almost be your strongest part of the climb. That could relate to the position of the climb within the sportive. Towards the end, you can afford to push a little bit harder, but if you're at the early stages of the climbs you want to be able to pace it really evenly. One way of looking at it is if you're approaching a climb in a certain gear and you're on the flat and you're going along at a certain speed you don't want to try and keep that speed as you take the climb, so try to measure it in perceived effort. If you're tapping along on the flat with an effort of Zone 3 then you want to keep that effort as 3 through the climb, whether your speed slows down or not. It doesn't make any difference, but if your perceived effort goes up to Zone 5 and you're keeping the speed high you're going to suffer later on.

Focus on YOU

Every climb you do you're going to get practice on so as time develops you'll become confident in your own climbing technique, and you'll adapt to what you've been doing over a period of time. With every climb that you do, try and think about the process of how you're climbing and what you're doing, rather than what other people are doing around you. You'll almost always get someone in a group who's stronger than you at a climb but if you're the strongest rider there, you're not necessarily the strongest climber in the world! So I'd think about the processes and technique of the climb and the way that you would approach the hill rather than who you're up against.

Again, relaxing your body is important and the steeper you go, the more you should think about balancing your weight towards the back of the saddle so that you're not leaning too far forward. This is the perfect time to get used to using your drops, so that you can lower your position on the bike and increase your stability. Make sure you're happy with your reach on the drops so you can cover the brakes.

As with cornering, keeping your eyes up and looking ahead to where you want to go is important, and stiff, sudden movements are best avoided. Clamping the brakes with white knuckles will just make things feel more jerky so let yourself go a bit, and use the brakes evenly to keep yourself at a comfortable pace. Look out for drain covers or pot holes, especially in the wet, but be careful with how far you pull out to avoid obstacles due to any passing traffic.

SIX MONTHS TO GO

DESCENDING
THE BASICS

When it comes to descending a lot of the same rules apply as when you're nailing your corners. Confidence is key, but never forget safety.

If you're lucky enough to be spending any time abroad with the bike, in France or Spain for example, you will have the perfect opportunity to dramatically improve descending in a short period of time. Long alpine-style descents give you the chance to see far ahead of you to gauge any traffic, which tends to be sparse the more remote you go, and practise picking up speed. After a week of coming down the mountains you'll be shocked at how confident you feel simply because you're riding every day, on the type of long, winding roads you rarely get in the UK.

If you're doing all your training on home soil that's absolutely fine. You'll need to build things up by trying to incorporate a range of gradients on your rides, starting off gently.

Coach's perspective

British Cycling talent development coach John Scripps gives us his top tips for descending like an expert.

I've seen people end up in the ditch for the reason that they perhaps lose their nerve. This is a common way of getting it wrong because if you lose your nerve or you snatch on a brake your wheel can lock up and you'll end up in that ditch. As soon as you've got a locked up wheel you don't have control of the bike. So the key thing really is to keep the wheels rolling and use the brakes to scrub off the speed. We all make mistakes in the beginning – I can say I've probably got it wrong a few times myself in the past, and as soon as I've put too much brake on it takes you straight off the line and the bike takes you where it wants to go rather than where you want so make sure you always have control of the bike.

often be surprised at the gains you have made overall.

Where are you now?

It's now crucial that you examine your time management. How is your schedule working out? Be honest with yourself. If you are constantly picking up colds, losing motivation or becoming overly tired, decide whether this is due to overtraining, being a tad lazy or burning the candle at both ends. If you want to achieve your goals, you must keep your eye on the ball.

If weight loss was your original goal check your vital stats as well as the number on the scales because you need to account for muscle mass. Take on board your body composition, so try to measure your fat percentage. Alternatively, how are your jeans fitting? Are they getting looser around the waist? This is a good test to see if you're going in the right direction. As you move forward try to avoid weighing yourself every day. Instead, once a week at the same time of day is a better indicator.

THREE MONTHS TO GO

SELF-ASSESSMENT

You're now at the three-month stage and we hope you're feeling fit and fresh, if so, well done and keep up the good work. But don't panic if things haven't gone to plan, we've got tips from the top to help you refocus and catch up.

Grab the list you made three months ago and refer back to where you were. Even if you've suffered with illness or slacked off from a few sessions, you'll

Up to you

We advocate self-responsibility within British Cycling. It is quite obvious – we can see the riders who have gone out and put the hard work in compared to the ones that haven't.

**John Scripps,
Talent Development Coach, GB**

Coach's perspective

Jason Cattermole is a coach for British Cycling. He explains why it's important to check you've put the building blocks in place before advancing.

You've got to walk before you can run and the more complicated stuff just won't make sense if you're not confident in the basics. There's no point in moving to the next level yet if you feel that way. There's also little point in doing really extreme training drills if you haven't got the basics right because it's not going to be of any benefit – it could even be of detriment. If you can ride safely and efficiently in a group, that will be one of the biggest boosts to your performance. Check if there's a velodrome near you as the skills sessions are accessible and extremely useful for building confidence.

Skills: the basics

By now you should be able to get up and over a hill at your own pace without cursing, and cornering and descending shouldn't fill you with dread. If you don't feel like you're at this stage, have a think about why not. It's a good idea to keep a diary, make notes and continue to work on your confidence before trying to push to the next level. Take your time and if you're not happy you've nailed the basics, schedule some skills sessions and go over things again. It's also an idea to get a friend that you trust to come out riding with you because this can help your confidence.

Field test

Has the time it takes you to do your field test improved? Is your heart rate coming down more rapidly after an effort? Are you getting up that hill in a faster time, can you complete 10 miles quicker than you could three months ago or are you able to use a slightly bigger gear for the same hill and still maintain the same cadence? Flexible indicators such as these rather than laboratory-style tests will help you determine at home if you are seeing the gains you desire. You should be seeing improvements in this area if you have been sticking to the plan.

Stay on the straight and narrow

If you're struggling with motivation it's a good idea to tell people, friends and family that you're in training. Not only does this mean that they're less likely to convince you to have that extra pint in the pub but it can provide a support network and that all-important accountability! Social networking has provided many riders with added drive because, when you tweet or update your friends on Facebook you'll have that many more people checking in on your progress.

Try for size

You should be starting to try out products, clothing and any energy fuels that you think you may want to use for the event day itself. That way you have plenty of time to gain confidence in your kit, and ensure that you don't have a brand-new and uncomfortable chamois or leave your stomach in distress due to a sports nutrition product that doesn't sit well.

Help from a coach

Commonwealth medallist, coach and all-round cycling expert Dave Le Grys gives advice for if you've fallen behind schedule or if you're starting your training with three months to go.

You've got two choices. If you're serious about completing your sportive, for three months out of your life, I think if you knock the drinking on the head, the socialising, and you think right 'just for three months I'm going to get myself into good shape' you can do it. Chunk it out so that you're doing, for example, a month of base, so long steady rides, nothing too hard intensity wise, and then the following month you can start building on that, carry on riding steady, but start including some harder efforts in that second month. Then on the third month, just do quality only so you might be training every other day, some good rides but loads of recovery, because it's the recovery that's going to give you that edge, that form. So just to recap, a bit of base, a bit of quality and then some really good top end. But in three months you've got to be looking at the bigger picture, in how you chunk that out. It's essentially the same as if you were doing it for a year, you'd do the same phases except you'd have more time.

THREE MONTHS
TO GO
ACHES

You've probably found out by now that cycling hurts at first. A few hours in the saddle is more than enough time to get a sore bum, a stiff back and aching muscles. But this is normal. If you put the body under any sort of pressure or intensity that it is not used to, you're going to feel a little sore. You're working muscles for longer than usual, and may be using some you've never used before.

When you look at your position on a bike, it's quite unnatural and there is a lot of strain placed upon your lower back and neck. Soreness is tolerable, providing it doesn't progress into anything else, so there is no reason why you can't keep on riding.

The aches and tenderness is actually a sign that your body is working and improving. It shouldn't be feared. Adequate rest will take care of this, and hopefully, should be less intense by the next time you go out and ride.

DOMS: A cause for concern?

Once you have returned from a hard day out in the saddle, you feel alive, and you're still running on the adrenalin and endorphins that are coursing through your body. However, once this has subsided, you get the exercise hangover, where every muscle in your body hurts to touch, and menial tasks such as walking up the stairs seem extremely daunting. But what is this feeling, and should it be a cause for concern?

Luckily, it's not a problem, it's just DOMS.

DOMS stands for Delayed Onset Muscle Soreness and is pretty much self-explanatory. It usually occurs 12 to 48 hours after exercise and is the body's response to extreme exertion resulting in muscle aches and soreness. In some cases the feeling has been so extreme that people have mistaken the discomfort for muscle pulls or even strains.

Although the research isn't completely clear on what causes DOMS, more and more studies point the finger towards the microscopic tearing of muscle fibres that occur due to intense exercise. However, some conflicting research claims that the discomfort may not be caused from the damaged muscle cells, but from the reinforcement process instead.

While there are some ways to reduce the symptoms of DOMS – none of which are scientifically proven – it is somewhat unavoidable.

Some people jump under a cold shower, some prefer warm baths, some believe an efficient warm-up and cool-down lessen the symptoms, while others opt for massage.

Whatever you try, remember that DOMS isn't a sign that your body is falling apart. It shows that your

Quick tip

If the bottom of your back is starting to stiffen, stand up on your pedals and ride for a few minutes out of the saddle. The pressure on your back will decrease.

body is working properly and is reacting to what you are putting it through.

Over the next few pages, we'll show you the best exercises to try to strengthen your body, and hopefully reduce the aches, sores, stiffness and tenderness that you may encounter when out on the bike.

Over the next few pages we will look at simple activities you can do at home to address the culprits of altered patterning, which will then help improve your core and enable you to develop a better cycling posture.

Weights and workouts

If cycling is your key goal there is little point in doing a traditional weights or gym workout if it doesn't transfer to a functional benefit on the bike.

That said, using weights does have some all-round conditioning benefits. Putting resistance on your bones helps to strengthen them, an important factor in preventing bone disease in later life. Using weights can help balance your musculature if it is done as part of a programme shaped to your needs. Body-weight exercises are equally as effective as machines or free-weights; and the squat, which we will deal with in the next chapter, is the most effective weight-bearing move for cyclists. It transfers well into power on the bike as it is a similar action to your movement as you attack, sprint or climb out the saddle.

Do I need to join a gym?

It would be better to use your available time getting in as much riding as possible. The off-the-bike exercises in the next chapter can all be done at home and if you want to add weights to your routine some simple dumbbells would allow you to add weights without the hassle and expense of joining a gym.

THREE MONTHS
TO GO

BALANCE AND CORE STRENGTH

To be a person with all-round fitness you need to consider what kind of exercises you do away from the bike to help keep your muscles and body balanced.

Most of us are only bike riders for a few hours every week but regularly adopt similar positions to cycling with our other activities, such as working at a computer or driving. Prolonged flexed postures cause muscle tightness and weakness and can have an influence on our overall strength.

Looking at how your muscles work, and strengthening those that need it, will help improve your functional fitness in all areas of your life. It will make you less prone to injury and ultimately help your performance on the bike too.

The dynamic core

Anne Dickins is a chartered physiotherapist and competitive cyclist, who has raced at the 2010 World 24 hour Solo Mountain Bike Championships. (www.oxtedphysio.co.uk)

Cyclists commonly suffer from deactivated, weaker cores (the muscles which support the spine) because on the bike they are held in a flexed position, which means that the body weight is supported through the hands and pelvis rather than through the spine, and the cycling movement involves unnatural, fixed, repetitive linear patterns. This weak core equates in cycling terms to pushing through a rubber crank – no point in a strong leg if is attached something bendy.

We spend a fortune on carbon-soled shoes but ignore the obvious: unbalanced muscles. Cycling in this way is very inefficient and predisposes you to injury. However calling it 'weak' is not quite correct; unbalanced and poor control is actually a better way of explaining it. Building up your core rarely requires sweat or grunt work as it is likely to be lying dormant and simply requires reactivation.

Most people think that stomach crunches, press ups (and variations thereof) will improve your cycling core. This is not strictly true. In order for your core to help in cycling, or any sport, the core has to work specifically in sport-related patterns in conjunction with the limbs. If the limbs work as an extension of the activated core it makes the limbs effectively stronger. When was the last time you required a press-up on the bike?

*There are **two basic types of muscles**, the ones that hold you – **the core** – and the ones that move you – the **limbs**. In cycling, the core has to be able to hold a constant but dynamic contraction to keep your spine still, while the leg muscles contract and relax as you push on the pedals. The ability to do this well this is what I call an effective dynamic core.*

*It is very common for cyclists to be unable to hold their core, breathe deeply and activate the limbs appropriately. It is usual for them to subconsciously bring in other muscles to substitute and assist in supporting the 'weak' core during exercise. I call this **altered patterning**. The common culprits are weak abdominals, outer gluts and the stabilising back muscles with over-dominant outer thighs and tight hamstrings, anterior hip, neck and shoulders. Hence a lot of cyclists suffer from knee, back and shoulder pain. A weak dynamic core will also cause you to rock on the saddle and cause your knees to wobble or drift in.*

As you can see, 'strengthening' your core to improve your cycling is not as simple as looking up core workouts online or doing a class down the gym. It is about working out which muscles are the 'weak link in the chain' in order for you to perform specific cycling dynamic core exercises. There should be no breath holding or altered patterning. If you are able to improve your dynamic core, it will make you stronger, more comfortable and more efficient on the bike. Using your muscles properly, without compensations, has the same effect as turning lights off at home when they are not needed – it saves energy – helping your riding to feel easier and ultimately for you to go faster.

THREE MONTHS
TO GO

BALANCE AND CORE STRENGTH EXERCISES

Here are key exercises that Anne Dickins suggests every cyclist should add to their training.

'These exercises are more about retraining your brain than about getting sweaty. A hard concept for cyclists to understand! They should all be performed perfectly since you are trying to retrain the muscles to work properly in cycling-specific movements rather than simply reinforcing old patterns. Do as many as you can do up to 30 reps. But if you can only do three before you substitute in your back, outer thigh or shoulder muscles then stop at three. The next time try and do one more. Build up in this way until you get to 30.

'The exercises should never be painful. If they are, or if you struggle to recruit the correct patterns I suggest you see a professional who can give expert advice.'

Clam

Purpose: Helps prevent rocking hips, knee drift, aids spinal stability. Prevents muscle imbalance across the knee and therefore pain.

Targets: Gluteus medius activation. This is not the best exercise for gluteus medius strengthening, however it is excellent for activating the inhibited gluteus medius in cyclists without the outer thigh assisting. Remember: most cyclists commonly suffer from thigh dominance. This exercise can be challenging as the outer thigh will try and overpower the weaker outer hip.

Starting position: Lie on your side with your knees bent up as in the picture.

One arm stretched out under your head in line with your straight back. Your top hand resting gently on your hip. Make sure your shoulders, hips and heels are in a straight line, your ribs are not flaring out and that your top hip is directly over your bottom hip by creating a small gap in your waist.

Action: Gently tighten your tummy below your belly button to help stabilise your spine.

Breathe in, and as you breathe out lift your top knee off the bottom knee (using the muscle underneath the place where your back pocket of your jeans is) keeping your heels together. Lower the knee and repeat. Both legs should feel exactly the same and you should be able to lower the knee without it juddering. You should feel this muscle contract as you lift, place your top hand there if you struggle to feel it.

Precautions: You should feel the muscle contract under your back pocket only. You shouldn't feel anything in your thigh, front of your hip or in the lower leg.

Avoid holding your breath. The only movement should be your thigh opening. Do not let your hips roll backwards or your back arch.

Squats

Purpose: Helps facilitate the correct balance of muscles across the hip and knee to the foot to prevent knee drift and knee pain. It will also help increase pedalling power and efficiency.

Targets: The glutes to fire appropriately in relation to the quads.

Action: Stand in front of a mirror with your feet a crank's width apart and your spine neutral, as in the photo. Align your feet so they are facing the way they would on your bike. Then make sure that your kneecaps are facing the same way as your feet. You may need to wear your shoes to achieve this.

Imagine that your legs from the knees down are set in concrete and are therefore immobile. Bend your knees, dropping your bottom down as if to sit on a low chair. Make sure that the knees don't move forward at all or turn inwards as you go down – they should point directly forwards.

Bending your knees, go as low as you can while still keeping your balance and your toes easily on the floor. As you stand up squeeze your buttocks together while checking in the mirror that your knees remain in line with your feet at all times.

Precautions: If this exercise hurts your knees – stop. It is critical to retrain your muscles keeping the correct alignment between your knee and foot so always do it in front of a mirror or reflection in a window (see page 68).

Variation: Once you have mastered the double leg squat try lifting one leg up first and doing a single-leg squat.

Purpose: Focuses on the ability to push down with one leg while maintaining a still back, enabling more power to go through the cranks.

Targets: Gluteus medius to retrain single-leg stability with the spine.

Precautions: Your alignment is even more critical in this exercise. As a test, lift one leg up but make sure that you don't shift your weight sideways at all. If your weight does shift, you are not ready to do a single-leg squat. Return to the clam, double-leg squat and modified bridge (see page 68) until you no longer shift before attempting this exercise.

Superman

Purpose: This exercise targets spinal stability so that when you move your hands from the bars you are able to maintain a still back and smooth pedalling. It also will help with sore hands, rocking pelvis and tight shoulders. The leg superman helps to open up tight anterior hips.

Targets: Core control, shoulder relaxation.

Starting position: On all fours in a box shape. Make sure your hips are directly above your knees and your shoulders are above your hands. Relax your shoulders but don't sag between your shoulder blades. Bring your shoulders away from your ears. (Rest on your fists if you have sore wrists.) Make sure that your spine is in neutral as in the picture below.

Action: Engage your core by gently bringing your tummy button closer to your spine. Keeping your belly button and nose completely still over imaginary dots on the floor breathe in and as you exhale raise one arm so it is level with your head. Hold for three seconds then lower. Repeat on the other side.

Precautions: Don't hold your breath. Don't shift your weight from side to side. Don't let your hamstrings contract as you lift your arm. Keep you spine still and keep your shoulders away from your ears.

Variations
Starting position as above.

Superman leg
Action: Slide one leg out behind and lift it to the horizontal.

Targets: Glutes, abdominals, spine stabilisers.

Precautions: Make sure that you don't shift your weight or rotate your spine to extend the leg. Keep your lower abs working to make sure you do not arch your back. You should feel your glutes, abs and opposite hip working. Keep your shoulders away from your ears.

Full superman
Targets: Global stabilisation.

Action: When you can achieve 10 reps of the arms and legs try raising the opposite arm and leg together. Hold for 30 seconds. Lower and repeat the other side.

Precautions: Make sure that you don't shift your weight away to one side and that your back doesn't twist or arch. Keep breathing steadily and keep your shoulders relaxed.

THREE MONTHS TO GO

PAIN

As we mentioned earlier, any sort of ache that is tolerable on the bike is fine and shouldn't do too much harm. However, the moment it crosses over into pain, then we need to take notice.

Soreness is one thing and pain is very much another and people often get the two confused. If something does feel painful, and you feel it is getting worse, you may have picked up a niggle. It's imperative that you keep a close eye on it and watch how it develops. If the pain doesn't subside, stop riding and seek some medical help. Pain is a signal that something is wrong. Don't ignore it. If you do, it could get much worse.

Exercising on a minor injury more often than not is the catalyst to developing more serious injuries. Most people will feel something, perhaps in their upper leg, and ignore it and continue to ride. What you may not realise is that with every pedal stroke you are causing more trauma to that area, thus increasing the likelihood of an injury.

Types of pain

Nociceptive pain
This is the pain that results in us letting out a squeal – it's an immediate, sudden response.

Non-nociceptive
This pain makes itself known via the nervous systems and occurs when nerves become trapped or damaged. This pain takes shape in the form of numbness, tingling or burning sensations.

As you haven't identified it, you may get home and rest for a few days. But unlike soreness, this won't go away unless treated. The symptoms might, but the root remains. So when you go out again, the whole process continues.

Back and knees
Although injuries can occur any place in the body, for whatever reason, for cyclists the two most common places where aches and pain occur are the back and the knees.

Being hunched over the handlebars for a few hours puts a lot of pressure on the lower back, which at first is tricky to get used to, as is the constant turning of the pedals for the knees.

This feeling for both is a dull ache, which although doesn't hurt constantly nags at you. You should find that when you stop, so does the nagging. However, if it's still hurting after a couple of weeks, then there may be a more serious problem that will need addressing.

A lot of people incur injuries on the bike but ignore them. This may be because often the pain isn't as severe as with impact sports, where broken bones

Four-point relief plan

If you do finish a ride with any sort of niggle, follow this four-point plan to help reduce the pain.

1. Ice the painful area for 10 minutes.
2. Rest for the next two days and repeat the icing procedure three or four times a day to ease inflammation.
3. Gentle stretching and massage will help alleviate tension and stiffness in muscles.
4. If the problem persists, monitor what provokes it and alleviates the pain, and seek help from a sports injury specialist or physiotherapist.

Short-term inflamed tissues or joints will respond to ice, Ibuprofen and rest. You should find that these problems will recover quite quickly. The next step is to see a specialist. Noting down your symptoms will help a therapist identify emerging chronic problems that could develop into more serious issues, preventing you from riding.

and torn muscles are the norm. You may feel physically fit enough to carry on riding, but your joints might not be able to, thus making a bigger problem for yourself, which you may be unaware of.

The key here is at first, to not overdo it. You should aim to increase your total mileage by no more than 10–15 per cent a week. Once you become stronger, then you can push the body harder. At which point, you will understand your body more.

Over the next four pages we will introduce to you a variety of experts who can help alleviate almost any pain or injury you may have incurred when on the bike. We'll let you know what they do, what to see them for, and when to go and see them.

Which expert? The basics

Dr Roger Palfreeman was Team GB's Team Doctor for over ten years. He currently practises musculoskeletal and general sports medicine and is team doctor for the Rapha Condor Sharp Professional Cycling Team. Here is his lowdown on what cyclists should be aware of, what injuries to look out for, and how to lower the chances of picking them up.

Firstly, if you do incur a pain, it's not just a case of going to see an expert. It all depends where the pain is. For example, there are certain areas that point more to bike fit. Pain in other areas could be down to shoe pedal interface. But it really does depend where it is, who the cyclist is and the nature of their symptoms.

The most common pains a sportive or new rider will incur are knee pains, which are usually related to the kneecap part of the join or the associated soft tissues.

Saddle injuries are common, which can be just things like saddle sores, but also problems with compressions of the nerves within the saddle region. Back pain is not uncommon, particularly if you don't have your bike set up properly. Also, people new to cycling will incur problems with compressions of the nerves in the hands and the feet. They're the most immediate things. Sometimes it's muscle pain that cyclists feel, such as muscles that are overused. They may not necessarily be muscle tears, but there will be uncomfortable sore areas within the muscles due to them being overactive.

Get your saddle right

One of the most important things for any cyclist is to get your saddle height right. People don't and get used to riding with an inappropriately low or inappropriately high saddle height and after a while it almost feels normal.

If your saddle height is too high, you'll suffer from back pain and saddle injuries due to more pressure. If it's too low, then you increase the chances of knee pain. Another really important aspect is getting the shoe pedal interface sorted out. That is largely a function of choices in terms of pedals, and to an extent the cranks. Get a good set of pedals, and set them up correctly and comfortably.

Also, be wary of saddle tilt. Get one that is padded at the front third or two thirds of the saddle because that's where the body weight sits. You load the front of the saddle far more than where your seat bones are meant to be. Set your saddle inclination for that first third of the saddle – 1–2 degrees of backward tilt.

If you wish to see an expert, make sure they have knowledge of cycling and biomechanics.

Saddles come in a wide variety of shapes, width and padding with different designs aimed at men and women, however that is not to say a woman will feel uncomfortable on a man's saddle or vice versa. The important thing is to find a shape that fits your own anatomy and unfortunately this is primarily down to trial and error. If you struggle to be comfortable try a wide variety of saddle shapes till you find one that fits you.

Which expert? Physiotherapists

Michael Crebbin is a chartered physiotherapist specialising in the assessment and management of cycling-related conditions and was selected to work as a physiotherapist during the London 2012 Olympic Games.
www.cyclephysio.co.uk
www.complete-physio.co.uk

What is the fundamental role of a physiotherapist?

Restoring normal balance and function of the body. Helping the patient reach equilibrium for the body, so everything can function optimally. Correcting biomechanical issues, weaknesses, stiffness, and asymmetry within the body does this. But we also promote independence and self-management. We don't just look at rehab. We focus a lot of our attention on pre-hab where people want to become stronger or faster. It's also a proactive way of addressing and knowing issues before they go wrong.

How important are physiotherapists for cycling?

Physiotherapists with an understanding of the biomechanics of cycling are very useful. We assess biomechanical riding position and issues with the musculoskeletal chain. We try and optimise and correct this, whether that's intrinsically by providing exercise prescriptions or manipulation. Or externally, such as bike-fitting and cleat choice and alignments.

When is it best to see a physiotherapist?

I'm not saying physiotherapists are better to treat injuries over other practitioners, but generally we tend to look more at knee pain and lower back pain, which is often related to biomechanical factors. Cyclists don't tend to get acute injuries unless they fall off, so what we see is biomechanical issues occurring over a period of time. It's then down to tweaking the bike and the rider to meet a happy position.

When should I start taking notice of the warning signs?

I would like to see people before they have to stop riding. The earlier you see someone the better before things start exacerbating. I would always advise people to see an experienced professional who has knowledge in cycling. Never self diagnose via websites and forums. And don't wait until your performance is impaired. If you are getting something that is repeatable – a consistent niggle – which isn't settling, then seek advice. If it's muscular ache from a new exercise, then give it time to adjust.

How can I spot a good physiotherapist from a bad one?

Word of mouth is always useful. Reputation often exists around experienced practitioners. By the end of the first assessment you should have a clear understanding of what is going on, what you want to achieve and where you are going. It may sometimes take two sessions to get to the bottom of a complex issue. If you're not finding the results you want, go and find a second opinion.

Which expert? Chiropractor

Matt Rabin is the Garmin Barracuda chiropractor and has been working within professional cycling for over five years. Matt was also only one of six chiropractors invited to the London Olympics.
http://theperformancechiropractor.com

What is the fundamental role of a chiropractor?

Chiropractic is a hands-on profession that treats biomechanical problems to do with joints, muscles and tissues predominantly of the spine. We find out what is wrong with the individual biomechanically, what's wrong with their joints, issues with range of motions, mobility and stability, and try to address these issues in order to get the body working back to its full potential.

How important are chiropractors for cycling?

It all depends on the outcome you're looking for. Should every cyclist see a chiropractor? In my opinion if you can ride a bike and you can get out of it what you want without causing harm, then no, a chiropractor isn't necessary. Most of the time pain is what drives people to seek help. If you have no pain, then there is no need. However if you're riding a bike and you feel pain, or if you get off and something isn't quite right, then it's probably worthwhile finding out where these irritations are occurring.

When is it best to see a chiropractor?

My job is to help the person. If someone comes to me and their issue is out of my range of practice, I will send them to someone else. If I feel I can help, then I will. If you have an issue ask a friend or a clubmate, and see what they did. Get recommendations. We're here to help, like in any other profession.

When should I start taking notice of the warning signs?

If you're a sportive rider and you've spent a fair few quid on your bike, your clothes etc. it makes logical sense to invest in your body as well. If you have consistent niggles when riding then I would invest in seeing an expert. I've seen very small issues neglected which have turned into major problems. Don't risk it, especially as you've probably got a set goal you want to achieve. If you feel something, take notes. Does the pain stop once you get off the bike? Does it linger? Is the pain progressing? Is it re-occurring? This all builds a bigger picture. Treat it early before it manifests into something that will stop you from riding your bike for a significant amount of time.

How can I spot a good chiropractor from a bad one?

Recommendations are the best port of call. Good reputations travel fast. If you can't find that, do some research online. Trust your instincts. If you feel your treatment isn't going the way you want it to, ask questions. Ask them how they can help and when you can expect to see outcomes. Who else have they treated? They're the experts. They should be able to answer your questions.

Which expert? Osteopath

Torben Hersborg specialises in sports injuries and sports performance enhancement as well as structural treatment for acute pain and long-term conditions. Torben has treated a wide array of cases that include World and Olympic champions. He has also given postgraduate lectures for osteopaths in German and Norway. www.londonosteopath.com

What is the fundamental role of an osteopath?

An osteopath will look at developing the optimal function of the body, examining the whole body and in particular the spine, before treating it. Where there is stiffness of the joints or muscles, we will try to free them up with the use of various types of manipulations, some slow and rhythmic and others fast, which give a click as the joint releases. We often use soft tissue work and trigger points (massage points that can affect a local area of the body by releasing specific nodules in that muscle). Some osteopaths use other methods such as cranial osteopathy, which is extremely gentle and works on the body fluids.

How important are osteopaths for cycling?

Osteopathy for cycling can be very beneficial both for injury prevention, treatment of injuries and for helping performance. As we deal with optimising the function of the body and in particular its biomechanics, it is like tuning up a racing bike. You make sure that the wheels run as smooth as possible and there are no unnecessary restrictions in any of the moving

parts. *Why not do the same to the body that is pushing the pedals? That's what we help with.*

When is it best to see an osteopath?

If you have any pains or aches, then it's worth looking into seeing an osteopath. It is best to prevent minor injuries becoming major injuries. We also treat lots of patients who are recovering from injury.

When should I start taking notice of the warning signs?

If your body movements become restricted, or start to ache, then you should be wary. When you train hard prior to competition it is of course normal for your muscles to have a healthy ache, but if they don't get enough rest you can get repetitive strain injuries or tears – which occur when muscles haven't recovered in time for the next workout. Also, if your performance starts to drop off then that could be a sign of being run down, thus increasing the chances of getting injured.

How can I spot a good osteopath from a bad one?

All osteopaths are qualified, registered and safe. Some specialise in office workers, some in babies and mothers, and some in sports people. The best way is to get recommendations from other sports people or google 'sports osteopath' in your local area and check their profile on their websites. You can speak to them, or email them for your specific wishes and ask them if they specialise in what you are looking for.

Some carbohydrates from the foods we eat are stored in our muscles where it is known as muscle glycogen but this is only enough for 90 minutes of exercise. We also need to restock those muscle glycogen stores after exercise. On pages 88–89 we talk about convenient ways of consuming food and drink on the bike such as energy drinks and gels, on page 112 we look at the role of carbohydrate in recovery. However, before you start adding these to your diet we need to look at ways of getting carbohydrate from real foods in your everyday diet.

THREE MONTHS TO GO

REFINING NUTRITION

As your cycling increases and you become fitter you are likely to find your diet needs to be modified or changed. On pages 32–37 we looked at how to clean up your diet and make it healthier, now let's look at how to fuel your cycling more efficiently.

Energy balance

Now that you are doing a bit more regular exercise your energy needs will have increased slightly. During low levels of exercise, which we will refer to as easy or Zone 1, effort will be fuelled primarily by fat. Fat is an amazing energy store. We all, even the skinniest of us, have 10,000 calories or more of stored energy in our bodies that can be used to power our cycling, but only at the most sedate level. Once we get beyond the point where we can comfortably chat – Zone 2 effort and above – fat can no longer be processed fast enough to keep up with energy demand and your body will switch over to burning carbohydrate.

What type of carbohydrate and when?

Carbohydrate can be found in fruits and vegetables, grains, cereals, pulses, sweets and sugars. Different carbohydrates affect your blood glucose levels in different ways and eating the right type at the right time can change the way you feel. The Glycaemic Index (GI) measures your blood glucose level and every food has its own GI score. Foods that have a high GI affect your blood glucose levels rapidly, giving a sudden spike in the amount of available glucose in your bloodstream. Low GI foods release

Foods on the glycaemic index (GI)

Low GI foods
Ideal for the majority of meals and before exercise
Low-fat yoghurt, wholemeal pasta, noodles, dried apricots, apples, porridge, oranges, baked beans

Moderate GI foods 56–69
Useful before and after exercise, use sparingly at other times
Muesli, sultanas, rice, honey, raisins, weetabix, pineapple, digestive biscuits, wholemeal bread

High GI Foods 70–100
Ideal during and post-exercise, best avoided at other times
White bread, bagels, jelly babies, jacket potato, water melon, rice cakes

their energy more slowly so there is no sudden spike and energy levels are maintained for longer. Understanding GI can help you choose what foods to eat when.

Low GI foods work best for the majority of your meals and snacks. Their slow release of energy is good for your health, maintenance of your energy levels, your mood and prevents feelings of hunger. Research has shown that low to medium GI carbohydrates are the best choice before exercise. They raise blood glucose slowly and maintain it over a longer period so that you can exercise for longer before fatigue sets in. When choosing your pre-ride breakfast or a pre-ride snack opt for things such as porridge, a fruit and banana smoothie made with milk or peanut butter on wholemeal toast.

High GI foods release energy into the body rapidly. In normal situations this is not a good thing. Take for example the handful of sweets or sugary bun you might snack on at work when feeling tired. Almost immediately you will get a rush of energy, you may even feel nauseous because of it, but very quickly your energy levels crash, leaving you feeling more tired than before. Rapid peaks and troughs in your

energy levels caused by eating high GI foods are associated with bad moods, headaches, and long-term health risks, such as the onset of Type II diabetes.

However, high GI foods do have a role in the diet of regular exercisers. During exercise when your body needs more energy to be rapidly supplied, high GI foods are perfect for the job. Carbohydrate drinks and energy gels are all high GI. When you finish your ride and you need to quickly restock your stored muscle glycogen and provide an energy boost after hard exercise, high GI foods are perfect. Sugary cereals such as Special K, white bagels with honey or jam, milkshakes or banana smoothies in the first 30 minutes after exercise will quickly restock your muscle glycogen stores and make you feel better, plus they have a small amount of protein to help with muscle repair.

Increased need for protein
Traditionally, endurance athletes such as cyclists and marathon runners have put emphasis on getting enough carbohydrate into their diets and protein has been overlooked. Protein is seen as the preserve of muscle builders. However, this isn't entirely the

case, so as well as checking if you have enough carbohydrate in your body to fuel your cycling be sure you have enough protein to recover from it.

Proteins are part of every cell, tissue, and organ in our bodies. Body proteins are constantly being broken down and replaced, particularly if you are exercising regularly. Proteins are made up of amino acids, the building blocks of the human body. The protein in the foods we eat is digested into amino acids that are later used to replace these proteins in our bodies. There are 20 different amino acids that join together to make all types of protein. Our bodies can't make some of these amino acids, so these are known as *essential* amino acids.

Protein can be found in many different foods: meat, fish, beans, tofu, eggs and cheese, for example. Animal sources of protein are complete, they contain all 20 amino acids, but other vegetable sources are not. Vegetarians have to be particularly careful that they have a varied diet to ensure that they have adequate amounts of the eight essential amino acids. Quinoa and soy are both complete sources, so they are worth adding to your diet if you are vegetarian.

Protection: antioxidants

Regular exercisers and serious cyclists in training put their bodies through more stress and strain than your average sedentary couch potato, which results in more damage to their bodies. Antioxidants found in fruit and vegetables can help counteract the damage done to our cells due to the oxidative stress of exercise. They also help to slow down some of the signs of ageing, such as skin damage, and boost your immunity to illness.

To help reduce damage and help you recover quickly from your exercise choose foods with high amounts of antioxidant activity such as pomegranate, blueberries, kale, red apples, cherries and, rather deliciously, dark chocolate. As a rule of thumb the darker and more brightly coloured a fruit or veg the more antioxidant protection it offers. Omega-3 oils also play an important role so aim for a couple of portions of oily fish a week or plenty of nuts and seeds in your diet.

What to do?

If you have ridden solidly for a few hours or so you will have lost a fair amount of fluid. Consuming water will rehydrate you; however, if your ride is more intense, your body would've sweated more and you'll start losing many nutrients and electrolytes.

Electrolytes are vital salts such as sodium, potassium and chloride, all of which are extremely important to the body. They help keep everything running smoothly and aid with the functioning of the digestive, nervous, cardiac and muscular systems.

These need to be replenished, and water alone won't do. This is where sport drinks and in particular hydration-specific drinks come in very handy. They're low in calories as well as sugar, and contain all the essential electrolytes as well as some vitamins, making them perfect for long rides.

THREE MONTHS TO GO

HYDRATION

Hydration is something that often gets overlooked, as most people will solely concentrate on nutrition when riding a bike.

However, hydration is one of the major factors as to why you may blow up during your ride. It could also have long-lasting effects, some of which are potentially harmful.

Dehydration occurs when more fluid is lost from the body than consumed, which will result in an imbalance in important minerals such as sodium and potassium. Both of which are required for muscle and nerve function.

Even in mild cases, dehydration should immediately be addressed. Low fluid levels in the body can affect our concentration, reduce our energy, create muscle fatigue and, in some severe cases, prevent organs from working.

An expert's perspective

Andy Blow of ProHydrate has worked with numerous top-level endurance athletes. He shares his views on the importance of hydration.

Thirst is a reasonably good indicator of hydration. Now that doesn't mean you should definitely drink when you're thirsty, but you should drink regularly. There is no mathematical formula on earth that can tell you that you should consume x amount of millilitres per hour because variables change all the time, such as how well hydrated you are before you start. For example, if you're well hydrated prior to an event, you are able to lose a little more fluids. However, if you're riding a Sunday sportive having been out on the town the night before, and you're already quite dehydrated, if you drop another 2 per cent body weight then you might well knacker your performance. It's all depends where you started at. It's quite difficult understanding the true meaning of dehydration. It's really down to listening to your body.

What you must understand, is the importance of replacing lost fluids with the right amount of electrolytes. A lot of people will drink lots of water, and then you run the risk of people who are losing high amounts of sweat and sodium in their sweat getting hypernatremia, which is where you put loads of fluids in, but end up diluting the body's minerals. This happens more often than people realise and is why your sportive rider at the end of an event might get cramps and feel tired because they've diluted themselves by drinking a lot on a hot day. What they've not done is put sufficient sodium in their drinks to replace what they are losing.

Check for dehydration

Symptoms of dehydration are quite generic, such as fatigue, headache, and feeling off like you would have when you are having a bad day.

The routine I would recommend to follow is: check the colour of your wee. It should be pale in colour, not clear. If it's too dark, then you're dehydrated [see Armstrong Urine Colour Chart].

If you're riding for an hour, water is enough. Anything above an hour, make sure you pre-hydrate with a 500ml to 750ml of electrolyte fluid an hour and a half before you go. That tops up your tanks and gives the body a chance to absorb it and pee any excess out. After that, it's a matter of listening to your body and thirst. Never force down fluids. If you're really thirsty, then you're past it, and dehydration has set in. It's a long way back and you can't rehydrate quickly.

Taking the pee

Estimating hydration status can be done by using something called an Armstrong chart. This is a chart with eight different shades of pale yellow through to brown against which you compare the colour of your pee. A reading of 1, 2 or 3 indicates good hydration, 4 or 5 indicate mild dehydration and 6 to 8 means you are suffering from severe dehydration.

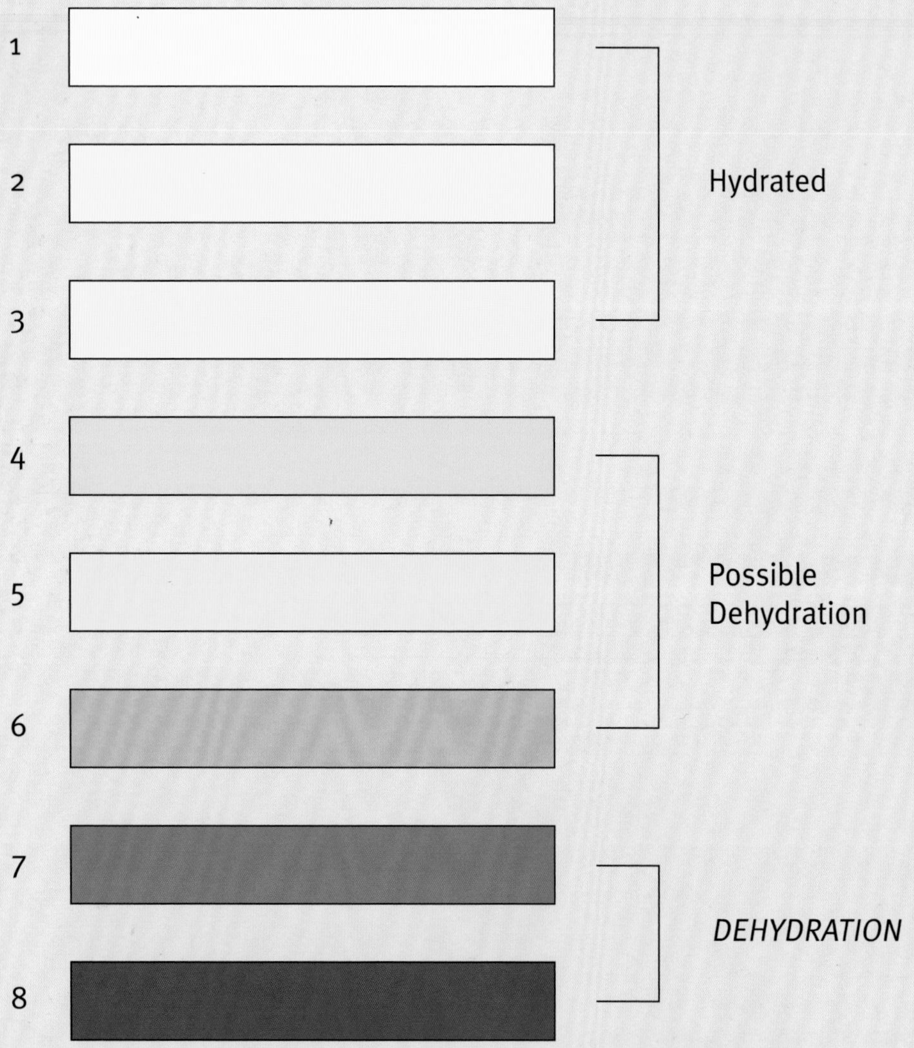

1

2   Hydrated

3

4

5   Possible Dehydration

6

7

8   *DEHYDRATION*

The Armstrong Urine Colour Chart

BEYOND FOOD

ARE SUPPLEMENTS NECESSARY?

Why take food supplements? Surely real food is far better? In a word, yes, real food is far better, but sometimes it isn't practical to gather the adequate amount of nutrients, minerals and vitamins from your daily diet.

Time is another factor. Fitting in your riding time around a hectic family life and busy work schedules can make it very hard to eat a rounded diet. For example, after spending an afternoon out in the saddle, the next step you must take is to refuel your body. You'll need carbohydrates to replace glycogen levels, as well as an adequate intake of protein to help rebuild your muscle and aid with recovery. However, you might not have the time to prepare a

rounded nutritious meal, let alone eat it, which could lead to illness and could even contribute to injury.

As you're preparing to complete your sportive, you want to be able to get the most out of your training. A bad diet will inhibit this. If you're not eating the right foods and at the right times, you are in effect starving your body of the vital nutrients it so desperately needs in order to maintain health and become stronger and fitter. This is where supplements can help. A big advantage of food supplements is that whatever you are lacking in your diet, you should be able to find a supplement for.

Have a sit down and look at your diet. Ask yourself what you're lacking. Can you get this from other parts of your diet? If not, what is the next step?

If you scour the Internet searching for the most beneficial supplements to take, you'll end up with nothing more than a headache and a confused look on your face. It can be easy to become too obsessed with supplements, and before you know it, you'll have a different pill for every day of the week. That's why we've spoken to nutritionist Mayur Ranchordas (see overleaf).

Advice from a nutritionist

Mayur Ranchordas is lead nutritionist for Team Rapha Condor Sharp. He tells us what we need to know about supplements, when we should take them and what to look out for.

You must get the foundations right. One of the messages we need to give out is that supplements are just that. They're there to supplement your diet. Our whole, real nutrition is crucial and then supplements such as gels, sports drinks and caffeine will be able to give you that extra bit (in terms of performance).

But the nutrition that you take in, day in day out; that's going to give you your 80 per cent gains that most people are after.

You need to take into account why you are taking supplements. Is it convenience, is it performance enhancement, is it recovery or is it some sort of deficiency in your diet? I always ask people that question. Why are you taking it?

Supplements fall into different categories. Gels, bars, recovery drinks and meal replacements are convenience foods. They help you out. Others, such as specific vitamins, are used to solve deficiencies. Then you have supplements that fall into the performance-enhancement category, such as caffeine, glucose fructose gels, beetroot juice and antioxidants.

It's worth noting that if you're taking supplements in order to enhance performance, then your best bet is through your diet. Elite athletes take supplement to gain that extra 1 per cent. But your weekend warrior will get bigger changes and gains through proper nutrition. Elite athletes are able to take these supplements because they already have well-rounded diets.

Err on the side of caution

When buying supplements, you must be wary. I spend the majority of my time dispelling myths and discouraging people from using supplements rather than encouraging them. There has been a big emergence of nutrition cowboys. Because supplements are a quick fix, you can make a lot of money from people who are driven and want to do well, quickly. Especially cyclists. More often than not, if you tell a cyclist to buy something and that it will make them stronger, they'll buy it. People are starting to realise this and are duping cyclists, which has resulted in an emergence of supplements that don't work.

Ask yourself this question: are they pushing loads of supplements? If the answer is yes, you can almost be certain something isn't right. If they're selling supplements to you, then that's a sign. And thirdly, if they've got a nutritional therapist type qualification, then chances are they're probably a crank. Remember: you want sports nutritionists and dieticians giving you advice.

BEYOND FOOD

TOP TEN DIETARY SUPPLEMENTS

Here are a selection of the 10 most-used supplements among athletes and non-athletes. We go through whether or not they're needed and, most importantly, how reliable they are.

Sports drinks

Sports drinks are by far the most popular supplement used by athletes. Isotonic sports drinks contain carbohydrates to provide fuel, water to rehydrate and electrolytes to replace salts lost in sweat. They have been shown to enhance performance and defer exhaustion. Recent research has found that when exercising for less than an hour, you may not need to swallow the drink. Rinsing the drink around the mouth and spitting it out has been shown to improve performance. However, when exercising for longer than an hour, consuming the drink is more effective.

Multivitamins and minerals

The use of multivitamins and minerals is very popular however, if you eat a well-balanced diet including five portions of fruit and vegetables a day they are not required. Certain sport vitamins can be dangerous as they contain mega doses of fat-soluble vitamins, which if taken daily can become toxic. Mega doses of vitamins should be avoided and general multivitamins may not be required if you eat a balanced diet. Make sure you choose a general multivitamin that provides no more than 100 per cent of the recommended daily allowances of vitamins and minerals. Rather than taking it every day it may be safer if taken every other day.

Caffeine

Scientific studies have found positive performance-enhancing effects of caffeine, making it one of the most popular supplements used by athletes. Most of the research has found that doses of 3–6mg per kg of body weight are effective. Caffeine taken around half an hour before exercise and during prolonged exercise can enhance performance.

Energy bars/gels

Energy bars and gels provide high glycaemic carbohydrate to the muscles, which is absorbed quickly. They are similar to sports drinks but don't provide the fluid. If you will be exercising for longer than 60 minutes then these supplements can be useful in providing additional energy. Most bars and gels are also fortified with vitamins and electrolytes which can be useful when exercising in the heat.

Protein supplements

You can now buy protein powders and bars in supermarkets and they can be a convenient source of protein. As most foods that contain protein require refrigeration and aren't always convenient, protein supplements can be useful. It is possible to obtain protein from the diet alone however, when travelling or having poor access to good-quality protein, supplements can be convenient.

Recovery drinks

Recovery drinks have become very popular as research has found that the quicker we consume carbohydrate and protein after exercise, the quicker our muscles recover. Most recovery drinks contain around 20g of protein and 40g of carbohydrate and are fortified with vitamins. However, a simple milk-shake taken immediately after exercise can be just as effective but much cheaper.

Vitamin C

Vitamin C supplements are very popular with both athletes and non-athletes. Most people take vitamin C supplements because they think it helps prevent illness (in particular colds) or alleviate symptoms associated with a cold. Unfortunately, the evidence supporting the use of vitamin C is poor and more recent evidence suggests that high doses of vitamin C may impair endurance-training adaptations.

Fish oils

Most of us don't eat oily fish such as salmon, mackerel and sardines at least twice as week therefore fish oils can be a useful supplement. Omega-3 is considered as a very healthy fat, and most of us could benefit from getting more of it in our diet. Fish oil supplements can be great for individuals that don't like oily fish.

Probiotics

Probiotics have been shown to reduce the incidence of traveller's diarrhoea and can be an effective supplement for immunity. Probiotics are good for gut health and some dairy products such as yoghurt have probiotics added. There does seem to be a benefit of taking probiotics and most supermarkets now sell probiotic drinks.

Glucosamine

Although the research behind glucosamine is equivocal it remains to be popular amongst athletes. Glucosamine is purported to reduce joint pain and stiffness however the scientific evidence is mixed. Some athletes feel that it is beneficial whereas others feel no positive effects. Glucosamine cannot be obtained from the diet therefore must be taken as a supplement. Some studies have found that it works because it acts as a placebo whereas other studies have found physiological benefits.

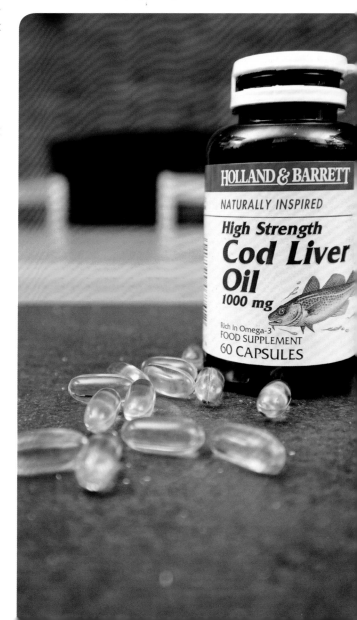

TECHNICAL NUTRITION

GELS/POWDERS/ BARS

While in an ideal world we'd have a chef providing us with real foods with the exact nutritional values we need when we need them, it often turns out that it's easier to grab a packaged product for instant benefit.

Science in Sport (SIS) founder Tim Lawson explains the science behind 'technical nutrition' and tells us exactly why we sometimes need to turn to gels, bars and powders for a more enjoyable ride and greater gains.

'The best way to think about your technical nutrition is not so much that it's just for the guys who are racing for the Olympic title or the Tour de France but if you're going to be riding close to your physical limits, that's when you can really benefit from technical nutrition. The other side of what you're trying to do with this kind of nutrition is to get the maximum amount of improvement in the shortest possible time. So if you think about your food on the bike, you want enough to be fuelling without unnecessary calories that may not help you to attain the body composition you want in order to go fast on the bike.'

Gels

'The great advantage with a gel, especially if you're trying to ride close to your limit, is they represent a technical way of getting energy in quickly and efficiently. It's going to be light on your stomach and enable you to ride close to your limit for longer. If you're looking for good adaptation and don't want to take on too many calories, you can always take an extra gel out with you, even if you don't intend to use it. It's always worth having an extra gel because if you don't use it this ride you can always use it next time. If you're on your way back and you're going a little bit further than you expected or you have a low patch then a gel can dig you out of a hole and get

you home in a whole lot better shape. If you think about it, most of us are in cycling for enjoyment so if you go out and blow your doors off it's maybe not altogether a pleasant experience. But if you've got that gel to top your energy back up it can make a big difference to how you feel.'

Energy bars

'The good thing about energy bars is you know what's in it, where it's come from and you can read the ingredients and find one that works for you. You carry it in your pocket, and it's great if you do have a café stop because it maybe means you avoid getting carried away. There's a big difference in calories between a whole load of cake and an energy bar! Often you've eaten a lot more than you need and, tempting as it may be, you get back on the bike and it can sit like a lead balloon.'

It all adds up

'In real-life situations around 80 or 90g of carbohydrate an hour will be the top end of how much you're likely to absorb in an hour. You need to add up what's in your drink and bars and anything else you might eat on the ride. You need to count all of that because if you're exceeding that amount it's more likely to result in gastrointestinal distress than improve your performance.

'Gauge what kind of session you're doing – if it's a long, hard session for you, then you might need to take more carbohydrate, but if you're riding with friends that are maybe not as quick as you, then there's no point in overloading on carbohydrate if you don't really need it.'

Caffeine

'Caffeine is interesting in that if it's before a short ride like a 10-mile time trial or something less than an hour it makes sense to take the carbohydrate and caffeine early because that will drive carbohydrate metabolism. However, if you're doing something a bit longer, then you want to preserve what carbohydrate you've got and try to work on fat. In this instance it makes sense to save that carbohydrate and caffeine gel until a bit later in the day and at least try to get a couple of hours in first.'

Zero-calorie drinks

'Doing some fasted riding with products such as Go Hydro, or similar calorie-free electrolyte drinks makes a lot of sense but can be overdone because this kind of riding is quite traumatic. If you're a newer rider I perhaps wouldn't suggest it.'

Recovery drinks

'I find it amusing sometimes when I see people after a mountain bike event maybe and they've got their highly technical recovery product in one hand and a burger in the other and I think, "OK, if you really, really want to eat the burger, every credit but at

Athlete's perspective

Joanna Rowsell, Team GB world champion and Olympic gold medallist explains the part in which gels, powders and bar play in her routine.

Energy and recovery nutrition products play a massive part in fuelling my training and racing as well as ensuring maximum recovery. It wouldn't be possible to continue to train hard day after day without them. I use energy drinks as well as bars and gels when I am training to provide energy. These are very important to keep me going on long endurance rides but also

on short hard sessions where you burn a lot of energy. Good energy drinks also contain electrolytes, which are very important to replace when you sweat a lot. Adequate fuelling during training also helps with recovery for the next day. A recovery shake made up of protein and carbohydrate straight after training is also a vital part of my routine. It is very important to get in some good-quality carbs and proteins as soon as possible after training as there is about a 20-minute window when these are best absorbed. A recovery shake is the quickest and most convenient way for me to do this.

I also try to ensure I have some normal food on the bike such as bananas. I think it is important to have a combination of energy products and normal foods as it is good to have variety. I would always have gels during a race but then things like bananas or jelly babies while out training.

On a couple of occasions I have got myself home using caffeine gels! It is awful when you run out of fuel, which is why it is important to start eating early on in a training ride rather than when you start to blow.

least give your recovery drink a chance." Your recovery drinks are designed to help you to refuel fast and help you to get the maximum adaptation from the exercise that you've done so they've got the right proteins, the right amino acids, vitamins and minerals. The electrolytes help to make sure that you retain the fluids and that you're not left

dehydrated so you really want to give that a little bit of a chance but for sure you need to account for the calories.

'By having a recovery drink, they work because there's a lot of thought gone into your various recovery drinks but the main thing is that you've got to plan a recovery solution, so you make your Rego up for example [SIS's recovery powder], put that in the fridge, or you know where your Rego is for when you come back. You've solved one problem because often if you come back from a ride you're hungry, and if you've not already planned your nutrition you open the fridge door and there's a bit of cheesecake left from the night before or some trifle, and before you know it, you've had 3,500 kilocalories and you only needed 300. If you have your recovery strategy, you've got your carbohydrate, you've got your protein – sometimes you might decide to have your protein and go easy on the carbohydrate but that's probably the most important thing, that you've planned it. You can do this with regular food but that needs a little bit more thought than just grabbing what's left over in the fridge.

'If you're starting your ride empty, you're almost starting your ride the next day how you finished your ride the day before, with a bit of delayed onset of muscle soreness on top of that. So if you're trying to do a quality session, or get the most out of your weekend you need to make sure you've stuck to your nutrition strategy.'

enough to flush it out. If you do need to remove anything from your eye, first take your gloves off and give your hands a quick rinse with plain water.

Injury to the head

Head injuries can be very serious and always need to be treated with caution. In the case of a severe crash or suspected head injury, immediately call the emergency services. However, if the crash is minor you may not realise that there has been a head injury. Paramedic Roy Wyle-Smith explains: 'When you injure your arm or leg the area visibly swells up. With your brain the swelling isn't so obvious because it is inside the solid box of your skull. What you don't want to happen is for a cyclist, feeling fine after a crash, to say goodbye to friends and driving home unaware that there is a bleed in their brain. Look at the helmet, if it is cracked in two or severely damaged it is worth getting checked out as that shows you have taken a hard impact. Consultants are always interested in looking at a cyclist's helmet as it can tell them where the impact was and how severe. Look at the mechanism of the injury: high-speed impacts are more likely to have caused significant injury. If you or a fellow rider feel nauseous, are actually sick, or vision is affected, or there is a persistent headache, or motor skills are affected making small tasks difficult make sure you seek medical help immediately. If a rider shows signs of

THREE MONTHS TO GO

FIRST AID

Road cycling isn't a particularly high-risk activity, however accidents do happen so it's important to know how to look after yourself and others.

Stings

Bee and wasp stings are surprisingly common as insects often enter through the vents of your helmet or down an open jersey. If a bee stings you, remove the stinger as quickly as possible to help reduce the amount of venom that gets into your skin. Ice can reduce the discomfort and swelling, as can anti-histamine creams or tablets. If you have an allergy to bee or wasp stings make sure that you always carry your epi-pen on rides and that your ride companions know how and when to use it.

Protect your eyes

Regardless of weather conditions you should always wear glasses to protect your eyes from grit or insects. However, even with wrap-around glasses you can occasionally get something in your eye. Your eye will naturally start to water which is often

A common break

Collarbones are one of the most common breakages in cycling as the impact is often taken through the shoulder or an outstretched hand. Thankfully collarbones heal quickly and have few complications. Bradley Wiggins, George Hincapie and Lance Armstrong have all suffered collarbone breaks and quickly returned to racing.

Paramedic's perspective

Roy Wyle-Smith works as a state registered paramedic and has over a decade's experience of working in the Emergency Pre-Hospital Care Setting. He is a member of the Cycle Response Unit and is an active British Cycling Coach and a partner at eliteVELO LLP, Fitness Consultancy and Cycle Coaching.

With proper preparation and good fortune you can enjoy a cycling career free of major injury. That said, accidents do happen and fortunately the majority of cycling accidents I deal with involve soft-tissue injuries and skin wounds. Although painful at the time, appropriate first-aid care will promote a quick recovery and avoid any chronic complications. However, with increased speed comes the potential for significant injuries. The most significant injuries will result from a high-energy transfer to the head, chest, pelvis or major long bones. Quick intervention can help stabilise injuries, preventing deterioration and promoting recovery, essential skills that can be learnt and developed through a recognised first-aid provider. I also cannot emphasise enough how important a good fitting helmet is and how it could save your life. So always ensure you maintain good visibility, read the road ahead taking into account the changing weather conditions, and adjust your riding style, so you and other road users remain safe. Communicate with other road users in plenty of time and avoid riding erratically. Final thought is location, location, and location: research the route prior to the event so in the unfortunate circumstances that you require an ambulance you can provide an accurate location, which will ensure a prompt response and timely transfer to the emergency department.

confusion such as repeatedly asking the same question, 'Where am I? What were we doing? What happened?' they are likely to be concussed and need checking out.

Fractures

A fracture is normally suspected when there is a reduced range of movement, deformity, swelling or pain. The most common fracture cyclists experience is the collarbone. If you are struggling to lift your arm and are having to hold your elbow to stabilise your shoulder the chances are it is a broken collarbone and you need to get yourself to A and E. For open fractures, suspected broken pelvis, hip or femur it is best to call for an ambulance. Don't leave the patient alone unless it is essential to go and call for help.

Take responsibility

When you are out on your bike you may be a long way from help so you need to be responsible for your own health and well-being. Take with you any medications that you may need, such as an inhaler for asthma or insulin if you are diabetic. Let the people you ride with know this. If you do have a medical condition consider getting a medi-alert bracelet, there are several designs ideal for sport. If you do have a problem the medics treating you will benefit from the extra information to take the best action. Carry a mobile phone so that you can call for help. Make sure you are aware of where you are; carry a map or use a GPS device. If you have an accident, any delay in the medical services finding you can be critical.

It's almost useless to try and offer any advice on how to fall as crashes occur very quickly. You might if you are lucky spot the danger and have a few seconds to deal with it before the sickening realisation 'this is going to hurt' passes through your head. If you have the time or presence of mind

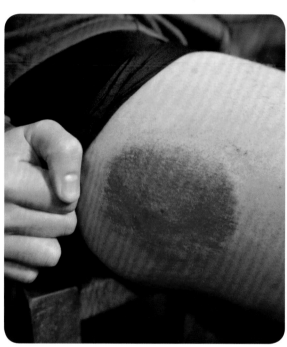

THREE MONTHS
TO GO

CRASH!

While crashing is far from inevitable it is a very lucky bike rider who gets through their whole career without falling off. However, the fear of crashing is often worse than the reality. Here, we run you through the steps you should take from the moment you find yourself on the tarmac.

Expert advice

UK domestic pro-rider, James Millard gives us his top advice on dealing with bike crashes.

Having come back from various crashes over the years I've managed to establish one thing: every single accident is completely different and needs to be judged individually. With most crashes the physical injuries quickly heal, however all of us battle with our sense of self-preservation in the months after an accident. I have found a few little tricks to help get over these nerves, if you're in a group with people you know try to follow someone you trust during the moments [in] which you find yourself struggling mentally, this will help speed up the process and bring you back up to your previous levels of confidence. Some take longer than others to get over but it helps to push the boundaries of your comfort zone within a safe environment when re-building confidence.

to do so, aim for a clear area where you are less likely to impact anything else and try to keep your legs and arms close to your body and chin tucked down.

Once on the ground take your time before trying to move. At this point if you are really badly injured then it is likely that the people around you will take over the situation. As with any accident the rules of first aid apply: if you suspect a head injury, if you have chest pain, shortness of breath or a broken bone that has punctured the skin you need urgent medical attention and should call immediately for an ambulance (see also pages 92–93). However, more often than not your injuries will be minor bumps and scrapes so take a quick mental screen of what hurts then get you and your bike to safety before doing anything further.

Once you are certain that your injuries are limited to road rash and bruises the best thing you can do is get back on your bike, ride steadily as obviously you will be a bit shaken but it will help prevent you from stiffening up and ease the shock of the experience.

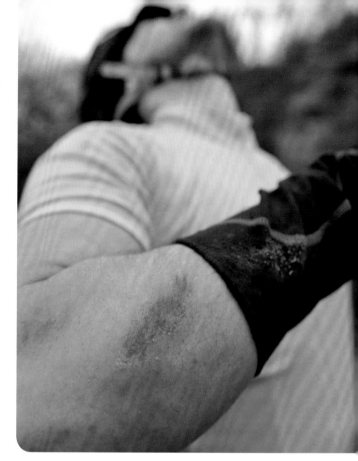

Treating gravel rash

Gravel rash is the most common consequence of a crash. While only superficial it can be painful, but as long as you look after the wound carefully and it doesn't get infected it is not serious. Here are some tips:

- Clean the wound as thoroughly as possible and as soon as you can. Do this by 'jetting' saline solution over the wound to carry away any debris without embedding it into the wound, then use sterile wipes.
- Once you've got rid of the visible muck, clean the wound and area around it using a mild antibacterial soap, a washcloth and lots of water. Then pat the wound dry. If there is anything embedded in the wound it is best to go to a minor injuries clinic where it can be removed properly.
- The best way of healing gravel rash is with a hydrocolloid dressing. Once applied you can leave it in place until healing has occurred. It'll drop off in a week or so to reveal new pink skin that will need protection from the sun. Keep a good supply of different hydrocolloid dressings in your race bag and medical kit at home.

Trust yourself and your bike; make sure you've checked your tyre pressure and quick releases before you go hammering into a fast corner.

Get used to cornering with others around you

On your own, you may have cornering perfected, but what about when you have the pressure of other riders preventing you from taking the line you want? It's worth considering how you may feel with someone on your tail or cornering next to you. Try to ride with friends or a local club to get used to taking a corner within a group. You don't have to push past your comfortable limit because you are not required to race round the bends, by any means, but building your awareness in this scenario is good for improvement and your happiness on event day.

THREE MONTHS TO GO

IMPROVING SKILLS

CORNERING

You should now be confident you can go up, down and around at a gradual speed without fear of slipping, sliding or panicking. Now it's time to take things to the next level.

You've probably got to the point where you've experienced a range of descents and if you feel you want to get even faster you need to identify where your weaknesses lie. Is it technique? If so, you could try placing a marker on the apex of the corner and practise your entry and exit line. Try this in an area with little to no traffic. If it's confidence at speed, practise the same corner 10 times, or as many as it takes to get it right, and hold your line. If you make sure you have plenty of room, in a park environment, for example, you can get it wrong and go wide without disaster, so keep trying – practice makes perfect.

What the pro says

Rapha Condor Sharp's James McCallum is known for his cornering speed on the professional race scene. He explains how to really nail your technique and how he handles things at race pace.

Think of a nice sweeping arc shape before you hit the corner. Look for a marker on the road that gives you a nice clean and fast entry point then do the same with apex. Keep on looking around the bend as you do so to spot the entry, apex and exit point. Relax your elbows and shoulders,

push down through your handlebars and put weight down through the outside pedal.

Make sure you brush off any excess speed before you lean the bike. If you have to brake midcorner you will defeat the purpose of coming in fast and lose all momentum you are trying to carry ... and probably slide out.

I always make sure firstly my equipment is in A1 condition, especially my brakes, wheels and tyres and I never enter a corner too hot not knowing what's coming up. My eyes are always 20 yards ahead.

The main benefit of good cornering technique is that you save a lot of energy. The more speed carried out of the corner the less you will have to accelerate to maintain you place in the group.

I always give myself enough room to run wide. You have three options: classic corner line (apex), defensive (tight to the inside to stop people out-braking you) and outside line (flowing). I always look to take the outside when in the bunch as it is usually the fastest, the inside line is usually full of people trying to move up by out-braking each other etc. This does mean that you have to come in a little later but you exit quicker.

comfort zone to move up to the next level. Good sportive times can really depend on your climbing speed so you can gain huge benefits from improving your performance on the ups.

If you find yourself easing back on the climbs and want to find more speed, hill repeats are a fantastic way to move on and up in your ability. On pages 103–105 we look at threshold and strength sessions. These will help improve your climbing by asking you to repeatedly climb a hill in a controlled way. Find a hill near to home so that you don't have a long way to ride back with tired legs. The challenge level of the climb is up to you, but as with everything it's good to build up gradually. If you have a group of riders you can go out with, it can be fun to race each other to the top to ensure you're putting everything into the effort.

THREE MONTHS TO GO

IMPROVING SKILLS

CLIMBING

When you first started climbing you probably found that just getting to the top of certain hills was a challenge, and for a lot of riders this is the toughest part of training. If you've been sticking to your plan over the last couple of months you should have already seen marked improvements in your climbing ability on your regular training loops and you're probably surprised at how much easier it feels in comparison to the first day you began the real training. As you keep slogging up the same rises, your body becomes more efficient, your muscles respond and your power increases. Now is the time to up your game!

You may find you can tackle any climb in a low gear with confidence and you will always make the top, so now is a good time to push yourself out of your

When you get to the top of the hill, the temptation is to ease back and relax but it will pay dividends to your fitness if you keep the gas on and push over the crest and keep the pressure on down the other side. You may feel sick, like it's too much hard work, or that you want to kick back but just a few efforts like this and it will all become easier.

We've all got a hill that we detest because it's just so hard but to step things up a notch you'll need to find tougher, steeper gradients and stop avoiding ones you hate. It's always good to get the legs spinning; massive gears aren't great for the knees but clicking down one gear on an ascent can really improve your power. Try riding in a slightly bigger gear on your regular hills and aim to get to the top in the same time. This will bring on your strength, power and fitness. And finally, refer back to your original field test times and set out to beat them. This will give a great mark of progress as well as motivation and focus.

Help! I'm not improving!

If you have experienced setbacks and feel as if the hills are still your enemy it's time to look at the reasons why you're behind schedule and be realistic in how to progress forward.

Excess body fat is a major factor in climbing because your lighter counterparts simply have less bulk to carry up the gradient with them and so you are working harder, burning off more energy and becoming more fatigued to sit at the same pace. This is why it could seem easy to keep up with others on the flat but feel like you're going backwards as the slopes kick up. You are not a full-time athlete and we don't suggest you dip much below 20 per cent body fat for a woman or 10 per cent for a man because this can affect your general well-being in day-to-day life. However, if you feel your weight is holding you back, refer back to the nutrition basics and be honest with yourself. Keep a food diary and make sure you're sticking to the right foods and controlling portion sizes.

IMPROVING SKILLS

DESCENDING

A lot of descending is about confidence and once you've built the solid foundations, it's about trusting yourself and the bike. Similar to cornering, looking far ahead is key to safety and competent execution so look at where you want to go and keep all movements smooth. Keeping your body relaxed, knowing where you want to go and retaining control will help you to enjoy the descents. When you've had some time to practise, descending can be the most exciting element of road riding and should be fun and time to let loose a bit!

Safety first!

Throughout the book we refer to ideal scenarios, but as most of us don't have the luxury of training on closed roads, you must account for traffic at all times. If in doubt, don't push it to your full capacity on a descent because if you hit a blind bend or a sudden string of traffic, you must be able to react in time. Pushing your limits on a quiet park road is ideal, but out on the open road you will need to make safety a priority.

Fitter, Further, Faster top tips

- Never snatch the front brake
- Try to gently kill speed in the approach to any bends
- Relax your body
- Let the bike flow on the straights but keep your weight on the bike evenly distributed
- Look at where you want to go
- Be aware of approaching traffic so as not to emergency brake
- Look out for other riders that may be overtaking
- Communicate as you pass others with verbal instruction
- Remember to enjoy it!

Athlete's perspective

Pro Tour rider Dan Lloyd has pushed to the limits during races like the Tour de France. He talks us through the dos and don'ts of advanced descending.

I've always been quite confident. I started riding seriously as a mountain biker, so I learnt a lot about how to handle a bike; I even used to do some trials riding back in the day. I learnt quickly because I started young, but that doesn't mean you can't learn to descend well even if you took up cycling a little later in life.

If things start to get a bit haphazard, I try to take a deep breath and think about my technique again. Like so many other things in cycling, you often go faster when you are smooth, as soon as you start getting ragged, everything falls apart and you are actually getting slower.

I would never encourage people to go beyond what they feel is safe when they are descending. We have to remember that pros are really the only people who get to ride on traffic-free roads, so safety always has to be first priority. But, if I could recommend anything, it would be to follow someone on a descent who you know to be both fast and safe – watch when they start braking, what line they take through the corners etc., you can learn a lot when you get to see things first hand.

few simple rules. This puts you in control and also teaches you the fundamental principles of how to tweak and manage your own fitness progression.

Quick tip

Go back to training basics (see page 41) for a run down on training zones if you have forgotten!

Key sessions
The long ride

Frequency: 1–2 times every 7 days

Intensity: Zone 1 and 2

Duration: 2–6 hours

Progression: Extend by 10 per cent every week, except rest weeks, up to 85 per cent of the total distance you need to ride.

Your first challenge when you start riding sportives is to make sure you can go the distance. Long rides challenge your endurance and get you used to sitting in the saddle for extensive periods of time. Your long ride needs to be at a steady Zone 1/ Zone 2, that means keeping the effort, not the pace, the same on hills and no sprinting for signs or racing your mates. Long rides need a lot of recovery so schedule a rest day after these sessions and pay particular attention to your post-ride nutrition.

THREE MONTHS TO GO

TAKING YOUR FITNESS TO THE NEXT LEVEL

With three months of solid base building and skill perfecting done it is now time to work on increasing your power on the bike, extending your endurance even further and getting some zip into your legs.

Creating a training menu

Everyone's lifestyle is different so a prescriptive training plan that demands you do such and such a session on a Tuesday or that you always do your long ride on a Saturday will work for very few riders. The solution is to have a menu of sessions that you use to create your own training week by following a

Cadence drills

Frequency: Once every 14 days

Intensity: Zone 1 and 2

Duration: 30–60 minutes

Progression: This session doesn't need to change but mix up the routines for your own interest. These are easy on the body so can serve as a recovery day between harder sessions. A smooth efficient pedal stroke is one of the signs of a good bike rider. It will save you energy and help you climb faster plus give you the change of leg speed needed for sudden accelerations or to sprint.

Threshold work

Frequency: 1–3 times every 7 days

Intensity: Zone 4 with Zone 2 recovery

Duration: 60 minutes–3 hours

Progression: Within a one-hour ride do five minutes in Zone 4 with five minutes' recovery, and repeat four times (20mins). Your next aim is 2 × 10 minutes

Power drills

Pedalling pyramid

Start in a gear that feels slightly heavy at 70rpm and then increase your cadence by 10rpm every minute until you reach 120rpm, then decrease by 10rpm until you reach 70rpm again. This is a power drill as well as a cadence drill because as you increase your cadence in the same gear your power output will also increase. This is a good drill to do on a turbo or rollers.

1 minute at 70–80rpm

1 minute at 80–90rpm

1 minute at 90–100rpm

1 minute at 100–110rpm

1 minute at 110–120rpm

1 minute at 100–110rpm

1 minute at 90–100rpm

1 minute at 80–90rpm

1 minute at 70–80rpm

Downhill sprints

On a slight incline, or with the wind at your back, change into a moderate gear that feels ever so slightly too big when pedalling at 50rpm (the big ring and middle of the cassette normally works). Jump out the saddle by pulling yourself forward on the bars and driving down hard with your lead leg, ride out the saddle for ten seconds and then, without changing gear, finish the minute in the saddle at the fastest cadence you can. Recover for five minutes and repeat. Do between five and eight per session. This will help improve your jump and your sprint.

Big-gear starts

Get into a big gear and roll along almost until you are at a standstill, jump out of the saddle using your arms and body weight to get the gear turning. Stay out the saddle for 20 seconds as you get on top of the gear and then sit down for 10 seconds aiming to hit 90–100rpm. Recover with fast, easy spinning for five minutes. Repeat four to six times in a session.

in Zone 4 with 10 minutes at Zone 2 between them. Then build up in five-minute increments till you have increased the amount of time working in Zone 4 to a maximum of 20 minutes non-stop. Do this for a maximum of 3 × 20 minutes in a three-hour ride. You should aim to increase your total for Zone 4 from 20 minutes a week to no more than two hours spread across three rides.

On the bike strength

Frequency: 1–2 times every 7 days

Intensity: Zone 2–3

Duration: 60 minutes to 2 hours

Progression: On a long, draggy hill select a heavy gear that you can turn at 50rpm and no faster. Ride for five minutes in the saddle focusing on maintaining smooth circular pedal strokes. Change into an easier gear and pedal fast for a couple of minutes and then repeat. Increase the number of intervals done per session to a maximum of 20 minutes in a big gear.

Power drills

Frequency: Once every 14 days

Intensity: Zone 5 efforts with Zones 1–2 for recovery

Duration: 60 minutes

Progression: These aren't strictly speaking Zone 5/6 intervals, they are more an evolution of your earlier cadence drills but they do bring in an element of sprinting and power. Cycle through the three sessions on offer and alternate them with your cadence drills to help train your brain/muscle connections to develop greater acceleration.

Recovery day

Frequency: 1–3 times every 7 days

Intensity: complete rest or other easy activity

Duration: 24 hours

Progression: none

Every training plan needs to include ample rest as it is during your recovery periods that you get stronger. How much rest you need a week depends on the rest of your lifestyle as well as your training. If you have a manual job that requires hard physical work you may find it harder to recover between training sessions so need more time between them. If you have a high-paced stressful lifestyle you may find that also hampers your recovery as it leaves you drained of energy. Ideally you wouldn't have more than three complete days off the bike per week. This would still allow a training session every other day which would be enough to keep your fitness moving forward.

Structuring your week

Plan your week in advance so that you know what you need to do daily and can be prepared for it. Here are a few simple rules to help you do this in the best possible way.

- Your long ride needs most recovery time so plan for a rest day after it.
- Strength days and threshold rides need most focus and commitment to do them well so plan these for days when the rest of your schedule is easier so that you have the mental energy to do them well.
- Cadence drills are easier on the body and the mind so use these on days when you are likely to feel tired.
- Plan your threshold ride for after a rest day or cadence drill so you are fresh for the harder effort required.
- If you are feeling too tired or short of time for a planned session try and fit in a 30-minute light spin or cadence drill instead.

Coach's perspective

Huw Williams is a British Cycling Level 3 coach who has worked extensively with sportive and road racers. He offers his advice:

Training menus are often more suited to the 'real world' than day-by-day training programmes. A pre-set training programme that dictates what you do and what day you do it on, doesn't take into account the myriad stresses and strains you'll be subjected to in your normal working day and the resulting cumulative fatigue that you accrue when trying to fit your training into an already hectic work/life balance. If a rider has an intense session scheduled for a certain day but is already heavily fatigued from the previous day's training and an unscheduled late-night work or family commitment that kept them awake half the night, clearly the rider isn't going to see the training response the session was aiming for. Indeed the training outcomes might not even be achievable in the first place. This leads to a highly de-motivated state as riders constantly find themselves missing training or performing below par when trying to shoehorn training sessions into a busy lifestyle. A weekly menu system where riders fit in a prescribed number of sessions around their weekly commitments is much more realistic, achievable and motivating.

- Don't ever try to make up lost time by packing in extra training sessions because you have had a few unscheduled days off. Just let those days go and get back to plan as soon as you can.
- If you don't have enough time for a long ride do an extra threshold ride.

This formula will work for training weeks of five hours up to 15 hours per week.

Planning your monthly cycle

Rest weeks or easy weeks are an important part of the bigger picture. We, along with most coaches, recommend a formula of three weeks training and one week easy. During the easy week cut back the volume of riding you do to 50 per cent of the previous week. If you did 10 hours in week three do five hours in week four. This will mean shorter rides and an extra day off the bike but keep the effort levels of your sessions the same to maintain your fitness.

Don't waste energy

Cycling is all about pedalling, the endlessly repetitive act of turning the pedals round and round, thousands of times each time you complete a ride of even a very modest duration. Consequently, any irregularity in the pedalling action that causes even the most minor loss of efficiency is magnified thousands of

times on every ride. You're simply wasting energy, risking injury and losing speed by not pedalling as efficiently as you might be. The main areas of concern are:

A) **Pedalling 'shape'.** Pedalling in smooth circles rather than a stomping, piston-like motion is more efficient.

B) **Pedalling speed (cadence).** Pushing too hard a gear for long periods places far more demands on the body than producing similar power in an easier gear at higher cadences.

C) **Pedalling balance.** The comparative power produced by each leg. A high discrepancy between right and left leg power output results in premature fatigue and overcompensation by the stronger leg.

D) **Simple,** single-leg pedalling drills and high cadence intervals done as part of the warm-up to other sessions will greatly improve your pedalling efficiency in all of the above areas and should be an integral part of any training programme.

Five golden rules for improving your fitness

1. *Hard and easy is the way*
Your body needs to be stressed in different ways to get the desired improvements in your fitness. It needs a combination of long, easy rides to build your endurance and develop your ability to use your fat store's fuel, and shorter, harder rides that will increase your speed, power and ability to handle lactic acid in your muscles. Riding moderately hard, for a moderately long time, does neither of these well.

2. *Don't neglect rest*
You'll often hear riders say that 'rest is the most important part of training' so make sure that you treat your rest with the same importance that you do your riding.

3. *Listen to your body*
Tuning into the sensations and feelings in your own body is an important part of training. You will learn to start picking up the signals that you are running out of fuel on a long ride and recognise the difference between fatigue, which means you need an extra day off, and lack of motivation, which just needs a good old kick up the backside.

4. *Consistency pays off*
It's not what you do some of the time that counts, it is what you do most of the time. One or two really good training sessions in a month is worth less than consistent week-in week-out riding. Try and keep an overview of what you are doing, building fitness takes time and you need to see the bigger picture to spot your progress.

5. *Focus on your weaknesses*
It is tempting to do the types of ride that you enjoy and that you are good at. If you like climbing hills you are likely to choose hillier routes, if on the other hand you hate climbing you may well ride out of your way to avoid a hill. Working out your weaknesses is a key way of improving your overall performance. Deliberately target your weaker areas and you will be able to turn them into strengths.

REST AND RECOVERY

As the days, weeks and months go by, our training starts to progress, our nutrition adapts, and our bodies start to improve. However, there is one thing that must remain the same: rest and recovery.

Yes, as we become fitter the time it takes to recover will shorten, but we shouldn't ignore or fail to understand the importance of adequate rest.

R&R is the key element in training, and if not done properly, will result in little improvement and could even contribute to deterioration in performance.

A common misconception is that the improvements in one's performance occur when out on the bike, in the gym, or on the weights. But this is wrong. Yes, this is where the hard work predominantly lies, but it is during rest when our bodies start to improve.

Rest to get stronger

Now when we say rest helps us to improve, that doesn't mean you can lounge on the sofa in the belief that it's going to help you ride your bike faster. Of course it won't. You have to put in the hard graft out on the road in order to push your body. But you have to give your body a chance to adapt to the stress you have placed upon it in order to progress.

To put it simply exercise breaks down our bodies and causes 'exercise trauma'. Working the muscles hard will result in microscopic tearing of the muscle fibres. We'll also lose nutrients and electrolytes and our muscle glycogen levels will start to run low. Our bodies will also have released the hormone cortisol, which puts them under further stress.

When you look at it like that, exercise doesn't sound too great. And you'd be right. It doesn't. Exercise is actually bad for the body. But doing the right things afterwards will help improve our bodies, making them stronger, fitter and faster.

Three-stage process

Many exercise scientists explain the process of improving in three stages. Body-builders know it as the adaptation principle, but the same process can apply to aerobic activity.

Stage 1: Trauma/overload (exercise)

In order to cause a physiological effect, we need to place a stimulus on the body. We need to work the body and gradually increase the workload to improve. Too much exercise, too soon will do more harm than good. On the other hand, if exercise is too light, then we won't cause enough of a physiological response.

Stage 2: Rest, recovery and diet

This stage – providing our bodies with sufficient rest and a nutritious diet – is the most important of the three steps, and is where our bodies will improve, providing we rest sufficiently and eat well. Without this, stage three cannot be achieved.

Stage 3: Adaptation

This is where we should see a difference, whether we notice our muscles becoming stronger and bigger or we see an increase in our speed and strength. At this point, our micro-traumas engendered in our joints and muscle tissue will have now started to heal and then the process can continue again.

This simple process clearly marks the route of exercise and progression and shows the importance of rest and recovery. Remember: without rest, the third phase cannot be achieved. If we ignore this, all we end up doing is breaking down our muscles further, putting them under more stress, resulting in a performance drop, as well as increasing the likelihood of injuries.

Diet for recovery

During exercise, the body will also start to decrease its rate of protein synthesis – the building of muscles – while increasing its rate of protein breakdown.

As well as resting, which prevents our bodies from breaking down further, we must eat. A post-workout meal high in carbohydrates is essential to replenish energy stores, and the extra inclusion of protein and amino acid solutions will help reverse this trend of protein breakdown.

In order to achieve this, we need to consume enough carbohydrates to release a significant amount of insulin. It is insulin that transports carbohydrates and amino acids to our working muscles, which will result in an acceleration in carbohydrate resynthesis. Our protein balance will also turn positive, which will help repair muscle tissue.

Athlete's perspective

Olympic track medallist, Craig MacLean knows all about the importance of rest and recovery.

Rest is more important than the training itself. If you're not getting decent quality rest then it's all a bit pointless. It's a classic symptom of the weekend warrior, they go out and smash themselves as hard as they can on the Saturday and Sunday and they never get the recovery quality they so desperately need due to work or other commitments. Recovery is everything. It's hard for normal folk to get full recovery. That's why professionals are in such a privileged position. What I will say is: if you have limited recovery time, you have to reduce the intensity or duration of your ride. Use some common sense and gradually build your riding rather than smashing yourself and pushing yourself into a deep hole.

Get the most out of recovery

There are many ways and tips to get the most out of your recovery such as cooling down, stretching, massages, or even opting for things such as ice baths or water therapy (the use of cold and hot water alternatively).

Our top advice as always is to listen to your body. Everyone reacts differently to exercise. If you're feeling particularly tired, rest, and take time to recover. If you're feeling strong, you don't have to force yourself to go slow if your body doesn't want to. Listen to your body and work with it.

But one thing you have to be careful of is overtraining. Overtraining, which we will look at in the next chapter, can cause major issues.

Food for recovery

There are many foods that work very well to aid recovery. We have chosen three that are extremely popular among cyclists, and they taste good, too.

1. **Chicken breast:** Packed full to the brim of quality protein to aid protein synthesis and complex carbs to replenish glycogen levels. Ideal to help build the body.

2. **Eggs:** Rich in branched chain amino acids. Perfect for protein synthesis. However, be wary of consuming too many due to its high cholesterol content.

3. **Tuna:** A quarter of a cup of tuna contains roughly 16g protein as well as omega-3 fatty acids, which help prevent protein breakdown and boost immunity while elevating metabolism. Not only that, but it's low in fat too.

Carbs vs protein

General academic studies suggest a carbohydrate intake of 0.8 to 1.2 grams per 1kg of body weight maximises glycogen synthesis although this does depend on the rigours of your ride. New research suggests that adding protein to a carbohydrate mix will enhance the release of insulin. The optimal carbohydrate to protein ratio for this effect is 4:1 – 4g of carbohydrate for every 1g of protein.

Do it like the pros

World and Paralympic champion, Jody Cundy:

Immediately after a hard riding session, I'll have a glass of cherry active juice as it's high in antioxidants and a protein shake to help repair the damage to my muscles. If I'm finished for the day, I'll usually have a pastas or rice based main meal, with lean meat and some mixed vegetables.

THREE MONTHS TO GO

BURNOUT

Overtraining is also known as chronic fatigue or burnout, and can best be described as an imbalance between training and competition versus recovery.

The biggest problem we face as cyclists who want to improve and get fitter is deciphering the difference between overtraining and feeling generally tired, and knowing when to call a halt to your training.

Cycling and fitness training in general can be very addictive once you get going, and many people find it difficult to stop. Especially when they feel it is something that is making them stronger, fitter or faster. This is where the problem lies. You must remember it's not the physical training itself that strengthens the body but the periods of rest in between.

A period of rest also gives you a chance to diagnose any niggles you may have picked up, and allows you to refrain from making them any worse.

However, none of this is possible if you aren't taking a break and it doesn't take a genius to work out the problems that will occur if you don't allow your body to recover.

In 'Does Overtraining Exist?', an article which was published in *Sports Medicine*, 2004, authors S.L. Halson and A.E. Jeukendrup stated that when a single training session is applied repeatedly with appropriate recovery, positive adaptation and improvement occurs. But if the balance between training and recovery is inappropriate, a state of overreaching may develop. If intensified and limited recovery continues the more serious state of overtraining may ensue.

But how do you know if you have fallen victim to overtraining? Fatigue in general is not a sign of overtraining, however, excessive fatigue is, but it's

not the only symptom. Here is a rundown on some of the main symptoms associated with overtraining.

Decrease in performance

This is one of the biggest symptoms associated with overtraining. Naturally over the course of a six-month training plan, we are going to have off days where things don't go right, or we simply can't be bothered. Such days are normal and you needn't worry about this.

However, if you're having trouble simply completing your normal workout, or you're struggling getting up the hill you ride every day, then you need to question why. We train to get better. But if training is having the opposite effect and our stamina is deteriorating and workouts are becoming much harder, then this could be a sign of overtraining.

Falling ill

Exercise causes our immune system to become susceptible to colds. Recent research has shown that those who compete in endurance activity reported a twofold to sixfold increase in the development of upper respiratory infections.

Sniffles, cold and coughs go hand in hand with cycling and isn't a cause for concern providing they are few and far between. However, if the frequency of infections rises, and develops into something more serious, or even if you take longer to shake them off, then you could have fallen into the trap.

Aches and pains

Once again this is totally normal, providing it doesn't continue for an excessive amount of time. As we mentioned earlier, the delayed onset of muscle soreness is expected after a hard workout on the bike. But if your muscles and joints feel particularly stiff, and it doesn't seem to be subsiding, then it may be more than that.

A good rule of thumb to follow is that grimacing to get out of your chair is fine but if you're struggling to get out of it then you may have pushed yourself too hard. If simple tasks like making a sandwich, or even getting into bed seem an effort too far, then you need to lay off the bike for a few days.

Sleep patterns

One of the great benefits from cycling is the long deep sleeps you fall into either on the couch or at bedtime. As we've exhausted our bodies we shouldn't struggle to nod off. So struggling to fall asleep after a long ride could be a sign that you have overdone it. This is because your body is still reacting to the stress that it has been put under through training and your heart rate hasn't lowered to its resting levels. Your sympathetic stress system is working extra hard to combat the body's reaction to exercise, both physical and emotional.

Mood swings

After a long session, exercise causes our bodies to release endorphins as well as adrenalin. Endorphins, which are also known as natural pain relievers, give the body a natural high, similar to that of what you would feel after laughing hysterically although this feeling is much greater and has been known to last hours and even days – another reason why exercise is so addictive.

However, if you have overtrained, these highs may be replaced with extreme lows and bad moods. You may find you become easily irritated and may even feel depressed. Remind yourself that exercise should lighten your mood, not put a downer on it.

These are just a few of the symptoms and one alone doesn't mean you have over trained. If more than two or three apply to you, then chances are the overtraining bug has bit.

An expert's perspective

Dr Roger Palfreeman explains there could be more to overtraining than just exercise versus recovery.

"Overtraining is all about how much stress is on that person and how they deal with it. It might be a case that the individual is training as usual, but has exams, and the combined stress of revising as well as training is too much to deal with. You then get a fatigued state where you are seeing demonstrable changes in performance along with a feeling of fatigue that won't go away with a few days of rest.

You've got to be tired, but you have to some reduction in performance to define it. It can be related to just training too much resulting in physiological stress. But in somebody else it can be down to stress in their relationship, workplace, exams and financial. It could even be down to dietary stress, where they're training the same, but are changing their nutrition in order to lose weight. Thermal stresses could also contribute. It's not just training. That's why sometimes people miss the point of overtraining, as it's not always about that. Of course training versus recovery has a huge influence, but there are also the psychological issues as well as medical issues. Once you have identified all of these issues, then you can start to find out what it might be that's causing fatigue.

If you're constantly tired or wrecked that's usually a good indicator that you've overtrained. Papers and research define it as a serious fatigue that doesn't resolve with two weeks of relative rest or a reduced performance in the absence of an underlying medical condition. Being tired for a couple of days isn't overtraining.

My top advice is to firstly rule out medical issues. Then rest. You don't have to refrain from riding, but rule out heavy training. In most cases, a few days off the bike will help. However, if two weeks of that doesn't reverse it, then you need to start thinking of other things. Remember, its not just training stress. It's a factor of everything.

"For those new to cycling, there is this belief that the more training they do, then the better they will get, which isn't the case.

Roger Palfreeman

THREE MONTHS TO GO

FAQ

It doesn't feel like I'm improving

Many people feel like this, but if you take a moment to see how far you have come, you'll be amazed at your progress. In sport, many people hit a performance plateau when on a training programme. This is quite normal, and is a result of your body getting used to the intensity you are placing on it. What you must do now is increase or change your efforts to provide new stimulus. Look at your training plan and find areas that need upping.

I'm struggling to eat gels

For some, gels are quite hard to consume, for some it's the taste, for others the texture of the gels themselves. It really is down to trial and error. Go out and buy a few and test them out on your rides. The health and fitness market is saturated with energy supplements so there should be one that suits your requirements. However, opt for gels from recognised brands, as some may be less effective than they claim.

My appetite is increasing. Is this a cause for concern?

This is perfectly normal and is a sign that your body is working and improving. All exercise burns calories, especially one as demanding as cycling. Energy needs to be replaced, and your body does a pretty good job at letting you know when it's running on empty. Due to the intensity of cycling, you are able to eat, lots. But make sure you are filling your body with healthy, nutritious calories.

I lack the power to get out of the saddle when climbing

Climbing out the saddle is less efficient than pedalling from a seated position as it requires more energy, however, occasionally you will need to have a bit of extra oomph to get up steep sections. Look at page 64 for dynamic core workouts as out of the saddle riding requires more upper body and core stability, and practise riding out of the saddle on the flat for several minutes at a time to develop strength and coordination. If it's your heart rate rocketing that is the problem, work on doing repeats of one-minute efforts on a short steep hill. If all else fails fit smaller chain rings or get a larger cassette, and find the right gear ratios that allow you to climb comfortably.

ONE MONTH
TO GO

it's common to experience lows such as a cold or feeling under the weather. Now is the time to avoid stressing about a sniffle and look at the bigger picture. Look at how far you've come and remember that a couple of days off the bike, or even tucked up in bed, will not undo your hard work. That said, refer to page 148 to ensure this final run up to your event allows you to avoid pitfalls and prepare you as well as possible for the task ahead.

Weight

If you've been targeting weight loss as an element of your training, you can still make gains in the final month but it is imperative that your body is not in a calorie deficit on the day of your sportive. Starving yourself in the final few weeks is not a good idea. Continue with your weight loss plan but be wary of fuelling in the final week. We will be covering your nutrition strategy in more depth within the next section, 'one week to go'.

Going the distance

Have you ridden 75 per cent or more of your event distance? You should be able to complete a sizeable chuck of the distance required by now, or at least be planning this in the next two weeks. It's important for your body to recognise what it's going to have to do on the day. If your event distance is 80 miles, this doesn't mean going out and riding 80 miles every day, as that will grind down your immune system and your body in the process. You simply need to ensure you've made a couple of your rides long enough to prepare for event day. If so, try to use the experience to think about what went positively and you'd like to replicate, and what perhaps didn't work so well. This is a great reference point for event day. Did you eat enough? At what points did you feel tired? Did you pace yourself well? Have a think about all these elements and use them to make sure things run smoothly for the sportive proper.

ONE MONTH TO GO

SELF-ASSESSMENT

ARE YOU ON TRACK?

Athlete's perspective

"You have ups and downs in training, and you can never be at your best all of the time.
Pete Mitchell, Team GB

We start this assessment with the wise words of GB sprinter Pete Mitchell because it's important to remind yourself that even the professionals have off days, and so will you. This last month is where you're going to refine your form and capitalise on all the hard work you've put in over the previous weeks.

When you start to back off from the really hard training and start to look towards your taper period,

The skills

Have a look at the course of your event. Check the gradients of the climbs and make sure you're happy with what's going to be required of you on the day. Take the time to familiarise yourself with the route and then go out and practise any areas of the key skills that you feel are your weakest.

Try, try and try again

By now you should be thinking about your nutrition strategy. Over the next couple of weeks, buy some extra products of the brand you intend to use for your event and try some out during training. Practise unwrapping a bar on the bike and see how your stomach copes with the foods you are asking it to digest on the move.

The clothing you began your training in may be completely different to what you'll need on the day so try to plan for likely weather eventualities and try to ride in these layers prior to the event so that you are not using brand-new kit on the day, which could lead to discomfort.

ONE MONTH TO GO

QUICK-FIRE FITNESS

Four weeks to go and you've only just picked up this book? Well, don't panic too much. There is a lot that can still be achieved.

Four weeks isn't very long to improve your fitness – in just a few weeks no amount of training will make an appreciable difference – but that is not to say 'give up and don't bother'. You can improve on where you are now and with a bit of solid effort and planning certainly make the experience easier and more enjoyable. Let's face it: doing something is going to be better, even now, than doing nothing.

Don't panic

Firstly a few words on what not to do. Resist all temptation to panic train. This is a well-known phenomenon when people suddenly get yanked out of their lethargy when they realise the event is only a few weeks away. Or worse, check their credit card receipt to discover they entered some horrendous 100-mile event after drunken bet one Friday (this scenario is more common than you might imagine).

The instinct in this situation is normally to dive in with a gung-ho attitude. Bashing out long miles, cleaning up your diet and doing intervals all at once is more likely to see you reach the start line on your knees with exhaustion or in the physio's room with an injury.

Plan wisely

Your first step is to work out exactly how much time you have available in the next four weeks. It needs a bit of juggling to carve out some time so be realistic but equally, as it is only for a month, be willing to make a few sacrifices. Split the time you have available into endurance, hill work and strength. Try and block some of your time together so you can do a good two- to three-hour ride once a week. 60/30/10 is a good way to split it, with the majority of your time doing long, easier rides and less time on hills or strength work. Plan one long ride of increasing duration with a couple of shorter hill sessions and two, short strength and cadence sessions. See pages 38–43 for details on these types of ride.

If you are suddenly increasing your training remember that your need for rest will also increase. For the next four weeks cut right back on late nights, stress (where it can be avoided) and other sports. Clean up your diet by getting rid of all the junk food and limiting your drinking to small amounts one or two nights a week. If you are going to see any improvements it will take some dedication, but remember it is only for a few weeks.

Plan the final week before the event to be an easy one. You won't need a long taper because training for only four weeks will mean you are fresh but a classic mistake is to keep doing long rides right up until the event. This will only tire you out. Your

longest ride should be in the penultimate week before the event, week three. Make this no more than 50 per cent longer than the long ride in week one otherwise it will take you too long to recover from it. Keep up the intensity by doing one or two short hilly rides early on in the final week but rest up for the latter part.

Sixty per cent of available time
The long ride
Frequency: 1–2 every 7 days

Intensity: Zone 1 and 2

Duration: 60 minutes–4 hours

Progression: Keep it to Zone 2 for the majority of the ride, take it really easy on the hills. Start with a distance that you feel comfortable completing. Add 10–15 per cent duration each week so that week three is no more than 50 per cent longer than week one.

Thiry per cent of available time
Hill strength
Frequency: 1–2 every 7 days

Intensity: Zone 2/3 and 4

Duration: 45–60 minutes

Progression: Either use a real hill or simulate it using your heart rate and effort levels on a turbo. Do a good 10–15-minute Zone 1–2 warm-up and then find a long hill, or change into a heavy gear that feels manageable at 60rpm, and ride top to bottom seated at 60–70rpm, keep your effort level steady by starting off easily and by the top you will be riding at Zone 4. Descend and recover then repeat but this time out of the saddle. Do this for 20–30 minutes then spin for another 10 minutes at Zone 1 before stopping.

Ten per cent of available time
Cadence work

Frequency: 1–2 every 7 days

Intensity: Zone 1–2

Duration: 45–60 minutes

Progression: Use the exercises on page 42-43 and alternate between all of them. Increasing your leg speed and developing your pedalling technique will really pay off given the short time frame. Plus these sessions are easy on your body so won't tire you out but will get you used to sitting in the saddle.

Training for hills when you don't have any

The turbo trainer is the flat-lander's hill session. Most long alpine climbs are ridden around Zone 3–4, which can easily be recreated on a turbo trainer. Start off by doing five minutes at Zone 4 with five minutes' recovery, aim to do four in a session, so 20 minutes total. In week three aim to do 10 minutes with five minutes in between three times, a total of 30 minutes. This is the closest you will get to re-creating the feel of an epic climb. Doing this is more valuable than targeting shorter, steeper climbs even if you have them available.

Coach's perspective

Huw Williams is a British Cycling Level 3 coach who has helped many riders reach their sportive and racing goals.

As a coach I frequently get calls from riders with only four weeks to get ready for a sportive with no real training in the bank. Here are a couple of things I've tried that have helped.

Treat it like a mesocycle

Mesocycle is a term used to describe a short (in this case four weeks) specific block of training aimed at accomplishing a particular goal (in this case your sportive). A typical approach is to spend three weeks building up volume before significantly reducing volume in the fourth week in order to recover. I've had more than one rider who's been short on training miles in the build up to a long event benefit from this approach, and it's amazing how much you can achieve in just a few weeks. It's a simple case of increasing your riding time day by day in a format of three-days-on, one-day-off, with a daily increase of just a few miles. Keep building your distance in this way up until week four, then cut the volume of each ride by about 25 per cent each day up until the middle of the week prior to the event, taking the last few days as complete rest to ensure you start with fresh legs on the day.

Face your demons

Sometimes the best solutions come in facing a problem head on. I once had a rider who simply couldn't climb hills, but had been press-ganged into joining a group of friends on a challenge to complete one of the UK's biggest climbing sportives. The rider in question was no stranger to regularly spending a few hours in the saddle, but would steadfastly refuse to ride even the shortest stretch of road when the elevation above sea level was greater in front of the bike than behind. He didn't thank me for setting him a four-week programme where pretty much every ride he completed was a sequence of climbs. On completing a climb he had two options, ride back down and climb it again, or ride to another climb close by and do that one instead. After four weeks of this the amount of climbing on the sportive was nothing compared to the amount of climbing he'd completed in training and there wasn't a hill on the course that held any fear for our man. Hardly the most scientific approach, but it was informed by one coaching staple: train your weaknesses, not your strengths.

REFINING NUTRITION

Choosing the right foods and fuels will help you get the most enjoyment and training benefit from every ride you do.

Your early morning ride to work
Before

Eating first thing in the morning is really important. Overnight the stored glycogen in your liver will be depleted by your brain activity as you sleep, so even though your body isn't doing anything your brain is still burning carbohydrate. Overnight you also lose a large amount of water through perspiration and mouth breathing so you need to rehydrate.

Ideally you would eat an hour before you get on your bike. Try changing your routine so that having breakfast is the first thing you do when you get up. The best pre-exercise breakfast is low GI, so a hearty bowl of porridge or muesli will provide the slow release of energy you need to get to work. Other good options are poached eggs or beans on wholemeal toast. If you don't have time to prepare

breakfast in the morning make a smoothie the night before that you can drink quickly. A yoghurt or milk-based smoothie with added fruit and honey will give you a good balance of protein and carbohydrate.

During

Unless your ride to work is longer than an hour you don't need any additional carbohydrates so soon after breakfast, however do make sure you drink water as you ride.

After

When you get to work it helps if you can have a small snack straightaway. This will help stave off mid-morning hunger pangs that might lead you in the direction of the vending machine or a biscuit packet. It doesn't need to be much: a piece of fruit with a handful of nuts, cottage cheese with oat cakes, vegetable crudités with hummus, or one of the less sugary cereal bars based on nuts, oats and fruit. Make sure that whatever snack you have is a mix of protein and carbohydrate.

Your weekend long ride
Before

If you are planning a long endurance ride of two to four hours or more, a solid breakfast is a pre-requisite for enjoying the experience, however you don't have to stuff yourself. Starting with an uncomfortably full stomach will lead to gastric distress as you won't be able to properly digest it once the ride is under way, plus you will be topping up your energy stores as you ride so there is no need to eat excessively beforehand.

As always, porridge and muesli are a good choice but if it is the weekend and you have a bit more time try a cooked breakfast with some healthy lean protein such as scrambled eggs on wholemeal toast. Make sure that you are drinking water or dilute fruit juice alongside that essential cup of tea or coffee.

During

If you are intending to be out for several hours it is important to start fuelling within the first 30 minutes of riding so that you feel strong throughout the entire session. Long rides are best fuelled with carbohydrate drinks and gels, ideally use the same foods and practise the strategies you intend to use during your goal event.

After

If you have been riding for a long time, even with proper fuelling, you will have used up most of your body's glycogen stores so the first thing you need to do is get carbohydrates in. The quickest and easiest way is with a drink, either a sports recovery drink or a chocolate milkshake or homemade smoothie. These options contain both carbohydrate to restock your muscle's glycogen stores and also protein to help repair muscle fibre damage.

It takes as much as 48 hours to fully restock your muscle glycogen stores after a long endurance ride. After a long ride you need to maintain your focus on recovery for several hours afterwards. Keep eating small snacks of high GI foods every two hours for the next four to six hours. Ideally they should be about 1g of carbohydrate per kilogram of body weight. For a 75kg man this would be a white bagel with a teaspoon of jam and a teaspoon of peanut butter.

Your 60-minute midweek session
Before
If this is an evening session you will need to start thinking about it during your afternoon at work. Nothing kills motivation for a training session like hunger and low energy levels. Plan a late afternoon snack for roughly two hours before you intend to ride. This also applies if you ride home from work. Go for low GI snacks such as fruit and nuts or oatcakes with peanut butter.

During
You shouldn't need to take on extra carbohydrate during a ride of just 60 minutes, however if you have got behind on your fuelling during a busy working day you may find that taking a caffeinated gel at the start of your session perks you up. If you don't like using gels then try a handful of dried fruit and a cup of coffee. Don't forget to drink plain water during your session.

After
Unless you are doing really tough intervals, 60 minutes shouldn't require a change of diet. A glass of water or a piece of fruit followed by a meal in the hour or two will be plenty.

A short sub-60-minute ride
Before
A short ride doesn't need extra fuel but you may find that you get more from the session, and may even burn a few extra calories, by having a strong coffee beforehand.

During
Keep sipping plain water.

After
As long as you have a meal planned within the next two hours there is no need for extra food now.

Your rest day
On your day off it can be easy to let your good resolutions to follow a clean diet slip. To a certain extent this is OK, even good, as it will help restock any deficit if you have been doing a lot of long or hard riding, for instance, a Monday after a weekend event. A day of eating slightly more than usual can also help boost your metabolism if you have been deliberately under-fuelling to lose weight, it snaps your body out of starvation mode where it may be hanging onto calories.

On your rest day your body will be repairing itself after the stresses of exercise so give it a helping hand with lots of fresh fruit and vegetables and high quality lean protein. Go easy on the carbs as they are really only needed as fuel for exercising.

Fitter, further, faster top tips

- Utilise your free time efficiently
- Schedule a session when you're going to have a chance to rest your legs afterwards
- Get out in your lunch hour, before work or extend your commute home
- If extra work or long-running meetings crop up reschedule your session and don't beat yourself up
- Don't allow one missed session to escalate into more

ONE MONTH TO GO

GET FIT WHILE YOU WORK

It's easy to make excuses when work is hectic, and while many riders struggle to find motivation to fit training around a busy day job it's surprisingly manageable once you get the ball rolling.

Time efficiency is the key when it comes to making the most of the hours you do have, and your energy levels will increase in line with the extra miles in the saddle, providing you rest and recover effectively from each session.

A desk job can make you feel lethargic but if you are essentially sitting down all day this can act as the perfect recovery from a morning or lunchtime ride, and if you're on the road or a manual worker a short run or trip to the gym can pay dividends. Once you've said no to a pub lunch or service station grub and switched it for a 45-minute spin session or an hour out on the road you'll find it increasingly simple to make this a part of your lifestyle. Getting your heart rate up in the middle of the day can help you to avoid that mid-afternoon slump and will reinvigorate you for the remainder of the working day.

That said, you'll need to factor in sufficient nutrition either side of your session to get the most out of the training. Having snacks and some recovery powder to hand can work wonders for impromptu rides that you haven't scheduled in. This means if the sun is shining, or you feel particularly up for a midday pedal, you will be able to get out, safe in the knowledge you can refuel when you're back at the office without having to run out for a fat-filled sandwich or fast food.

Recognising the difference between when you can push yourself through lethargy and laziness and when you're genuinely tired from a hectic schedule is important to avoid overtraining.

Rider's perspective

Rachel Przybylski, ride captain, for HotChillee events London–Paris and the Alpine Challenge, knows how tough sportives can be when you're riding long, back-to-back days. To be up to the job she has to be at peak fitness, while also managing a hectic job in the city.

My career is tough. Us city bankers work hard and put in serious hours: 7.30 to 18.30 Monday to Friday is standard. I find that many cyclists have careers like mine, our dedication to our job and our sport is at the same level: 110 per cent. It's tricky not to overdo it when I am fitting 60–90 minutes of exercise in either before or after work! That's why I have a coach, to tell me when to back off, and show me the best use of my time. Time is precious.

One option is commuting. I tend to ride with a fellow city worker (safety in numbers) and we motivate each other. We ride in steady and on the home leg it's all out up the hills … race time!'

I also make sure I get a good night's sleep, I eat well and I have regular sports massage and see a chiropractor. I do lots of stretching too. If you look after yourself you feel less tired, even if you really still could do with just a little more recovery. I never pressure myself to commute either. If I don't feel up to it I listen to my body and take a break. Maybe later that same day I'll get home and ride a static bike indoors, either a turbo trainer or a Wattbike instead.

I would advise riding with others or finding a club. I think getting quality training in is better than quantity. Yes, for long sportives you need miles in your legs but save the long rides for weekends when you can go with a group and learn road craft at the same time. Use the mid-week sessions to get fitter and stronger by adding in intervals or hill repeats, for example.

Excuses are usually born out of fear of hard work, which is almost always worse than the actual effort of training. Find a way for your sport to be your outlet. Riding in a group, giving yourself a social element to training and avoiding letting down people other than yourself will make you stick to your commitments.

ONE MONTH TO GO

TAPERING

Training provides the long-term fitness benefits you need to succeed, but in the short term it leaves you tired. As you get closer to event day it's important to back off from your training so that you can freshen up and remove the fatigue. The trick is finding the optimal balance between resting and training so that all you lose is the tiredness and not any of your hard-won fitness.

What are the benefits?

A paper published in the *International Journal of Sports Medicine* reviewed more than 50 scientific studies on tapering to find out whether it improves performance. Most studies found an improvement of about 3 per cent when athletes reduced their training before competition. When you ease off your training load slightly you are able to recover fully from your riding, your body is able to heal all the minor damage in your muscles and your fuel stores will be completely replenished. Research has shown that athletes, after completing a taper, are able to produce more power, their muscles are more able to cope with lactic acid, their blood volume increases and they have greater capacity to work hard on the bike.

How do you do it?

Getting the right balance is important, and as you get to know your body and do more events you will start to learn how long a taper you need. Some people seem to need longer than others. Several studies have concluded that the optimal length of taper is from seven days to three weeks, depending on the distance of the race and how hard you've trained. Too short a taper will leave you tired on race day, while tapering for too long will lead to a loss of fitness. A good rule of thumb is that the longer the event you are training for, the longer your taper should be because you will have more accumulated fatigue. If your event is 100 miles, start tapering two weeks before.

A taper should leave you feeling sharp and fast; the key is to maintain intensity but reduce volume. Cut your total mileage or time by as much as 60 per cent but keep doing the hard efforts and intervals. Just doing easy riding may seem like the best way to recover and rest but it will leave you lethargic and slow and if you cut the intensity you will lose some of your fitness. Where you may have been doing a two-hour ride with 2 × 20-minute efforts at just

below your threshold pace, during a taper you will do a one-hour ride with 2 × 10-minute efforts. Less time on the bike will reduce the strain on your legs and allow you more recovery time between training sessions but the intensity of the intervals will ensure that your muscles are still accustomed to going fast.

By the end of your taper period your muscles should feel full of 'pop' and 'zip', as if they are primed and ready for action. You won't feel tired or lethargic but alert, excited and ready to go. You may feel that you can ride harder and faster than you ever have before and your body will feel desperate to try it out. Often the hardest part of a taper is finding the discipline required to go easy when you feel so good!

What to expect

A taper can do funny things to your body and your head. When you are training hard and frequently your body is used to regular effort, so missing out on it can make you feel lethargic and heavy-legged. If

you are used to riding most days, keep doing so but cut right down on the volume, even just a 30-minute spin will help prevent these feelings from occurring.

You may find that you have a few more minor aches and pains than usual. These often emerge when the load is lessened early on in your taper period and will fade as your body heals and recovers. Some riders find that if they ease off too much they may start to get a scratchy throat or the sniffles – it is as if your immune system that has been working so hard to keep you healthy during your training to fight off illness has now eased back slightly. Keep looking after yourself with a healthy diet and plenty of sleep and it is unlikely those sniffles will develop into a full-blown cold.

Less training and more recovery means that your body is able to fully restock its energy stores (see pages 155–156 for advice on carbo-loading). As this happens your body stores water in your muscles alongside carbohydrate so toward the end of the taper you will weigh slightly more and your muscles may be visibly plumped up. Don't panic! This is good, it is the fuel you will be using during your event, not fat gained through inactivity. Having more stored carbohydrate in your muscles can make some riders feel a bit stiff or 'wooden'-legged. A quick cure for this is to jump on the rollers, the turbo or a flat bit of road and intersperse an easy ride with 30-second bursts of really fast, high cadence spinning – it will make a huge difference to how you feel.

As it gets nearer to event day you may start to worry that tapering has caused you to lose fitness or that you aren't as ready as you hoped. There can be a desire to do a hard ride and push yourself to see how fit you really are. Reining yourself in at this point can be difficult but it is important not to blow all of the gains from your recovery period in the final few days. You will still be doing harder efforts so listen to your body. It should feel as if you are straining at the leash to get going. When you are spinning gently on a recovery ride your legs should feel fluid, loose and fast. Trust that you are ready.

Coach's perspective

Mark Fenner is the coach and physiologist behind www.ftptraining.com. As well as coaching riders of all abilities he has competed internationally on road, track and mountain bikes.

As a coach, one of the most important considerations during the taper is the psychological well-being of the athlete as much as the physiological side of the taper. You need to keep the self-talk positive and resist the temptation to go out for longer than the schedule outlines. The head will be saying, 'You need to train more' or 'I will just add another climb, that will be OK, won't it?' However, your training is done, you are in great condition and it is now all about the taper. Manage your eating with what I call 'good fork control', as with the reduced volume you will not be using as many calories and it would be easy to regain that lost weight. And get to sleep early to avoid a late night.

By the end of the taper period you should be feeling ready to jump out of your skin. The sensations while walking up the stairs should feel effortless and while completing the designated training sessions there should be a feeling of fast legs and no chain on the bike. You may see a slight increase in heart rate for your perceived effort, but this just means you are fresh and ready to go. Think of this as the rev limiter being taken off your engine: you are now ready to go like a Formula One racing car.

NUTRITION

OPTIMISING AND MAINTAINING WEIGHT

Optimising and then maintaining your weight can be a difficult equation to balance, especially when you have a plethora of energy foods and sugary snacks facing you. SIS founder Tim Lawson talks us through some practical ways to look at gaining your ideal body composition.

Diet

'If you haven't previously used technical nutrition, you probably rely on convenience foods, which isn't always that great nutritionally, but it's got energy in it, so it will work to a degree. The problem when people switch to the technical nutrition is they continue with the coping strategies and the technical nutrition on top of their normal diet, that can backfire because you can take on more calories, you might

recover really well but it's perhaps not going to help your body composition.

'The biggest tip here is that when people take up cycling or sport they know that they need carbohydrate energy for their workout, the problem then is, they have the same kind of carbohydrate breakfast or meals when they're sitting in the office all day and you've got to ask the question "What are you going to do with all that carbohydrate?" So when you're not on a training day it's better to find some good-quality protein, for example, eggs and fish, and some real good fresh vegetables and fruit and reduce your consumption of rice and pasta. If you are doing a hard workout then have your rice and pasta but it's the time away from your training that you really want to restrict your carbohydrate calories.

'The other thing unfortunately is beer. Thirteen pints is about the equivalent of one pound of fat – you don't need to drink them all in one night but if you've got a big event, every 26 pints that you avoid between now and then could make you a whole kilo lighter. I'm not saying don't drink anything, but if you reduce your consumption then you would benefit, if all other factors remain the same.

'Try and think about a qualitative approach to food. Think in terms of "how much nutrition is there in here and does it taste fantastic?" rather than just, how much am I getting for my money. You can use a protein shake, mid-morning and mid-afternoon to take the edge off your appetite just so that you eat a little bit less at the meal that follows.'

Taking it too far

'The biggest problem when people aren't fuelled correctly is not necessarily that they get too thin but that they've depleted their glycogen stores when it comes to the event. You need to plan things out or you could turn up tired and without sufficient recovery. Sometimes you see riders in this state and they've just not eaten so they've missed the protein and carbohydrate after their rides and they're not fuelled up prior to the event, so they're not properly recovered. In those final two or three days of tapering it's best not to be in a negative calorie balance. You want to change your diet back to more carbohydrates so that at least you're starting with your muscles recovered and with a decent fuel store.'

Athlete's perspective

Moderation and balanced diet is the key maintaining a healthy event weight. A simple way is calories in versus calories out – it's the best equation, but common sense goes a long way.

James McCallum,
Rapha Condor Sharp pro team

Fitter, Further, Faster top tips

- Assess how much you want to lose and set an achievable goal
- Aim to lose no more than 2 pounds a week
- Be realistic about the number of calories you're burning off
- Don't base your body assumptions purely on the BMI scale
- If you stray from your plan, don't panic, but focus on getting back on track
- Don't scrimp on food when you need it most
- Find a mechanism to avoid boredom eating
- Reward yourself for reaching each weight-loss goal

Body Mass Index (BMI)

By simply taking your bodyweight and height into account the BMI scale is flawed because it doesn't account for muscle mass and fat. BMI can be used as a rough guide as to whether you are overweight but some Olympic athletes would fall into the overweight bracket due to their muscular build so don't fixate on this as a sole indicator. As an active person in training you will realistically expect to gain muscle and lose fat, but this could leave you at a similar weight, so it's important to look at your body composition rather than weight vs height alone. While calliper tests will best determine your body fat percentage, bathroom scales are available with functions to provide this figure as well as estimating your visceral fat (the fat around your internal organs), so these may be a useful investment if you're aiming to slim down ahead of your sportive.

ONE MONTH TO GO
PACING

Pacing is all about eking out your energy: too fast, too soon and you'll reach exhaustion before the line; play it too conservatively and you'll finish with the disappointing feeling that you could have gone harder.

Perfect pacing requires you to know your body and its capabilities, so practise your pacing strategy so you know the sensation of what a sustainable pace for you is, and it will help give you the mental strength required to stick to your game plan on the day.

Plan ahead

Perfect pacing begins with research. Take a look at the profile of your event and work out where the hard sections – normally the climbs – and the easier sections occur. Make a mental note of any descents where you will be able to recover a little bit and know where the tough bits are so you can mentally prepare yourself for them. You may find it helps to have the route on your GPS or mobile device, or even just have the profile of the course taped to your bars. Think about how you will manage your

nutrition. You should know where the feed stations are on the course so you don't run out of fluid. If there is a very long hard climb try and get a bar or gel in 10–15 minutes beforehand to give you the fuel to get up it.

Effort levels

Pacing is all about effort, not speed. Over the last few months you will have been training using effort levels so you should be familiar with how your body feels at each stage. An event of over an hour such as a sportive will be ridden mainly in Zones 2–4. If you remain within these levels and use good nutrition you will be able to sustain an even effort throughout the ride, and if you are riding to get a good finish time the majority of your ride will be in Zone 3. The challenge is to even out your effort across the route so that you push as hard on the hills as you do on the easier sections. If your effort level is too high on the flat when the hills become difficult you won't have any more to give. You may need to back off your effort a little on hills, particularly at the start of long ones, as this will raise your effort level into Zone 5, which will make it harder for you to sustain the pace: this zone burns lots of fuel and exhausts you. In the early stages when you are fresh and enthusiastic you may feel like you want to push on but consciously start off a little bit easier than your body wants to go. Holding back will ensure that you have something left towards the final part of the ride. Practise pacing on your long rides, it will help you start to recognise the sensations of trying too hard and overdoing it.

Use tools to pace yourself

If you use a heart-rate monitor or power meter in training then you may find it helpful during an event as well. For solo events you can stick very rigidly to a plan and having some numbers to watch will help you focus. However, if you are going to do this it is important that the plan you set yourself is realistic and based upon your best performances in training rides of similar length. Your heart rate is very unreliable as it is influenced by many things: at the start it may be high due to nerves and excitement, heat can also elevate your heart rate as can a phenomenon called 'cardiac drift', which is where your heart rate climbs higher as exercise goes on.

Many experienced riders choose not to look at heart rate or power as they prefer to go on how their body feels. If you feel good, are rested and your training has worked well you may be able to go harder than you expect, in this situation following the numbers may hold you back.

Expert's perspective

Mike Cotty is an endurance specialist and star of Cyclefilm's sportive guides and route reconnaissance DVD's. He has been the first British Finisher in L'Étape du Tour and La Marmotte.

I find that, for me, pacing has come with experience. The beauty of a sportive is that it's as much of a challenge within yourself than it is with the thousands around you. It's OK to push it into the red on occasion, to get into the group ahead or hold on to the summit of a col, but I'm always mindful to maintain a pace that I know I can sustain for the duration of the event. It's far better to finish strongly than on your knees.

Choosing when to work with other riders in a sportive

Working together with other riders can help the whole group travel faster while reducing your own energy expenditure. In large sportives, riders seem to naturally drift together into groups, so take advantage of this whenever you can. Getting into a well-organised pace line is one of the most enjoyable and rewarding experiences of cycling. If you want to get a really good time in an event this is a technique not to be ignored. However, when it comes to pacing yourself for a long event you need to keep your wits about you as there are several easy traps to fall into.

Firstly, don't put yourself into the red early on trying to stay with a group that is significantly faster than you are. It will feel good getting sucked along with fast riders when you are fresh and full of adrenalin at the start but if you are overreaching your capabilities and begin to struggle you may well end up blowing badly and finishing much more slowly than you would have had you stuck to a steadier pace from the start.

Don't get cocky if you think the group you are in is moving too slowly for you. Obviously you don't want to be held back by staying there but unless you are significantly faster you may find they catch you again quite quickly. If you made a big deal of attacking off the front this will make you look really silly. Instead try working out who the strong riders are and share the work with them, gradually upping the pace. You'll soon shed those who can't keep up but will hopefully keep some riding companions. Brutal, but that is sport.

Be fair in the amount of work you do on the front. This is a sportive not a race, there are no prizes for winners, so the tactics of sitting on and sparing your legs for a sprint is wasted here. If the goal of the group is to get the best finish time possible then working as a team will be better than the group disintegrating because of prima donna tactics. If you are struggling to do your fair share then say that and try to cling on as long as you can. If this happens, respect those who have done the work, don't sprint them and do make sure you let them know you appreciated the tow.

ONE MONTH TO GO

FAQ

I can't sleep, help!

There are many reasons why you may be struggling to get off to sleep. First check your lifestyle. If you are training close to bedtime or eating a large meal you may find your body temperature is raised and your heart rate elevated, making it harder to drop off. Make sure you have a good hour of wind-down time before hitting the sack. Try reading a book or listening to music instead of stimulating activities like television or computer use. A banana and a glass of milk before bed will release the feel-good sleep-inducing hormones dopamine and serotonin so think about having these as a late-night snack.

Is it harmful if I take a week out of my training plan so close to my event?

Having to take a break due to other commitments may worry you but it could prove helpful as long as you keep to your healthy diet and stay active. Try and ride a little bit if you can to keep your legs spinning and keep some harder efforts in to maintain your fitness but see it as rest that will make you strong for the event. Don't try and compensate for the week off either before or after it, just stick to your plan.

I'm starting to worry about the event. Is this normal?

If you have put a lot of effort into preparing for an event it is normal to want to do well at it and think about how that will happen on the day. That is a positive emotion. However, if your worry is feeling negative and it feels upsetting or overwhelming, take a close look at exactly what it is that you are concerned about. Write it down and see if there is anything you can do to address it. There may be practical ways you can address your fears. If your worry is about the outcome or whether you will reach your goals, remind yourself of how much you have already achieved and remember that doing your best on the day is the greatest achievement of all.

I feel like I'm peaking too soon

If it is the final two weeks before your event then this is the feeling you are aiming for. Stick to the training sessions and enjoy the experience. However, if you have a month to go, although you should feel stronger now than ever before you should reasonably expect to feel a little bit tired as well. If you feel really good now – and you haven't started tapering yet – add a little bit more distance to your long ride as your body can obviously handle it. A peak in fitness can be sustained for 2–3 weeks if you keep the balance of lower volume of training and high intensity efforts right.

ONE WEEK
TO GO

SELF-ASSESSMENT

You've got one week to go so now is the time to assess where you're at and keep your aspirations for the day realistic. You may have had the most perfect six months of your life on the bike or you may have experienced setbacks but now isn't the time to try to make big fitness changes as you will be entering into your taper period. Trying to dramatically cut calories or go out and train really hard will not benefit you at this stage. However, if you're feeling great then factor that in, plan to start near the front of the pack and take that confidence forward.

Knowledge is power

By now you should have looked at all the event information in order to start planning. Have you been sent rider numbers or do you need to pick it up on the day? It's a good idea to take a form of ID if you are picking up a chip on the day and make sure you know your start time and any other requirements.

Coach's perspective

World Masters Champion and Senior L4 Coach Dave Le Grys offers advice for riders who have filled out the entry form but for whatever reason have not managed the training they anticipated six months ago.

"The thing with sportives is that you can get carried away and go off with the big, fast guys or you can ride sensibly with a group that's riding at your pace. The way to think about it is that you need to play it smart – train smart, ride smart. So if I had let myself go before the big day and was going to panic, first of all I wouldn't panic. I'd ride that 20, 40 or 80km sportive but I'd ride with a steady group. I'd rather ride with a slower group and feel strong, than one slightly too fast where I'd get blown out of the back and feel demoralised in the state of mind that I'm in.

Diet and hydration

If you've been putting in the hard work to get down to your optimum event weight, the last thing we're telling you to do is kick back and eat a whole chocolate cake. It is, however, important to think about what you're fuelling your body with during this final few days. Tim Lawson of SIS explains:

'You see people who have the hydration message, so they're walking round with a two-litre bottle of water and they're drinking that much water that they're probably washing out a whole lot of their electrolytes before they even start and they'll be in an even worse state than if they'd just moderated it a bit. So I think on those few days prior to your big event the thing is to not go mad. You can go overboard eating too much so that you've put additional stress on your body, because it's got all this food that it doesn't quite know what to do with. You need to think about what you're eating and be a little bit sensible. When people say 'take 200g of pasta', it's not the creamy cheesy stuff, it's the pasta bit so don't go over the top with those excess calories. Celebrate your success afterwards but try and think of real quality this week.'

ONE WEEK TO GO

DON'T SELF-SABOTAGE

You've trained hard, eaten well, done your research and you're feeling ready to go, so make sure you don't mess it up. Trust us: there are plenty of experienced riders who have thrown it all away in the final few days.

Don't overdo it

There is little you can do now to improve your fitness but a lot you can do to damage it. Don't throw in a hard ride because you want to test your fitness or because you think one more session will give you the edge – it won't. Even if you think you haven't done enough training, don't bother doing any more now because going into an event fresh will give you far more of an advantage than an extra ride will.

Do pack your bags early

If you are the sort of person who normally leaves packing to the night before, on this occasion make the effort to do it early on. That way you'll be able to make sure all your kit is clean and ready. Go through the whole process of doing the ride in your mind from getting dressed. So that is shoes, socks, shorts, chamois cream etc. Nearly every event a rider turns up without either shoes or a helmet, which means they can't ride.

Don't be tempted to tinker

Even if the bike shop tries to sell you a new saddle or tells you the reach of your bike is too long do not change things. You will have got used to that piece of kit or position however right or wrong it is and you will almost certainly regret doing it as any change takes a while to get used to.

Do get some early nights

You might not feel so tired as usual if you have been easing off the riding as part of your taper but do try and get to bed early. Nearer the event and the night before you may feel a bit nervous and struggle to sleep so make sure you aren't carrying any additional sleep deficit.

Don't dramatically change your diet

With only a few days to go your focus should be on getting in plenty of good carbohydrates and eating well. Stick to foods you know and enjoy. This is particularly important the night before if you have travelled to a hotel as digestive problems can seriously screw up your event. It is a good idea to take a stash of food with you when travelling, especially if you have any food intolerances or allergies.

Do avoid people with colds or illnesses

It might make you look a bit anti-social but for the final few weeks try to avoid friends, family or work colleagues with any colds or illnesses. During a taper phase you can become very susceptible to picking up stuff and you won't have time to shift it before the event. It may sound neurotic but shopping online and avoiding shaking hands are two really easy ways to stay cold-free.

Don't try anything new

In the last week or so don't change your routine too much. If you've never had a massage before, don't book one now. It may seem like a good idea but you don't know how you will respond to it. Some people find it makes them heavy-legged. Same with stretching or training sessions: stick to what you know and what works for you.

Napping is also very good for the body, and providing it's no more than roughly an hour, it can be extremely productive. Research shows that napping can lower stress, increase alertness as well as increase cognitive functioning.

Massage

A massage is a great non-drug therapy that can help cyclists with sore, tight muscles. Research has also indicated that an efficient massage can help reduce inflammation in the muscles and increase blood flow. While there are many sceptics who still question the positive effect a massage has, it won't do you any harm, and if it feels good and helps you relax after a ride, then why not. However, as mentioned in the previous chapter, if you've never had a massage before, avoid booking one so close to the event.

THE IMPORTANCE OF TLC

Over the course of the last five months, you have made some pretty big changes to your lifestyle as a whole. Your daily activities have changed, your exercise levels have increased and your diet has been altered hugely. Although it's all for a greater cause, you have in effect forced your body to adapt, and pushed it to levels it may not previously be used to.

Now is the time to reward your body, or at least try and help it. With a month to go, your training should be heading in the right direction. To ensure it stays on this path, make sure you look after your body. There are many ways you can do this.

Sleep

Your body loves sleep. It helps restore energy levels, relaxes your body, and aids the recovery process after a vigorous day in the saddle.

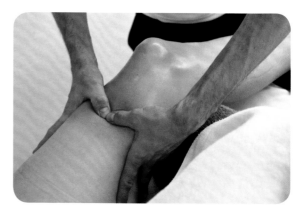

Cold baths

Love them or hate them, cold baths are proving more and more popular among those who endure long bouts of aerobic exercise.

The belief is that immersing yourself in cold water will help alleviate muscles soreness and inflammation. While the research isn't as strong as some other methods, there have been studies indicating their effectiveness.

Leg shaving

Now this might seem alien to a few of you but according to some people, whether you're a man or a woman you're not a real cyclist unless you shave your legs.

Some people believe it improves your aerodynamics, some say it's easier to treat road rash, while others believe that shaven legs makes massages more effective. The truth is, no one really knows. It's up to you. We won't force you.

Expert's perspective

Sports therapist and IG Markets Sigma Sport rider, Simon Gaywood offers some tender loving advice:

If you can afford it, I would say have a professional massage once a week, it gets your muscles in so much better condition. So if you can afford to have a massage just look locally, or at colleges as well, they often offer a service with their students that is checked and supervised by the tutors and you usually pay a fraction of the price as you would if you were going to someone who is fully qualified.

In between massage you need to stretch, but the newest thing is the foam roller. Everyone hates them but once you get used to them, it's similar to really deep sports massage. When you first use it, and you've got really tight IT bands and quads and things like that, it's horrible and really painful but once you have a few massages, or you've used the foam roller a few times, the muscles soften and they actually get used to the pressure. So I'd say if you can't afford a massage, get yourself a foam roller, it will cost you about 15 quid online and it will be your best buddy!

and question what it is that is driving us. More often than not, it leads to a feeling of deflation and results in many people giving up at the last hurdle.

With one week to go, your body should be in pretty good shape. Now is the time to switch the attention to your mind, your focus, and your concentration.

Mind over matter

The mind plays such an important role in cycling and could be the difference between success and failure. The moment the mind goes, it is very hard to get it back, and more often than not, your performance will suffer. Cycling isn't the easiest sport in the world, and at times it seems as if it constantly wants to break you. Staring at the proposition of five hours in the saddle can seem daunting. Combine that with rain and hills, it's no wonder that many people mentally break.

ONE WEEK TO GO

HAVE FAITH IN YOURSELF

We all have our own personal goals, which should've been set right at the beginning of our training. But there will come a time when your motivation is low, your drive isn't as strong and your self-confidence isn't where it should be.

These negative thoughts usually come towards the end of a training period, or when the event is fast approaching. We may start to doubt our ability, wonder whether all the hard work has been worth it

Have confidence

It can be hard to sometimes generate self-confidence, but the good news is that just like the body, the mind can be trained too. We may not possess the raw natural talent that top-class athletes hold in great abundance; we may never be able to sprint like Mark Cavendish, climb like Andy Schleck or time trial like Tony Martin. But we can learn the psychological skills that they have which enable them to perform at the top of their game.

One key psychological element that all top-level cyclists posses is self-confidence. Mark Cavendish is a great example of someone who holds great self-belief in his own ability. Some mistake it for arrogance, but it's not, it's total self-assurance.

With your sportive not long away you may start having thoughts of self-doubt, or negative energy as some people call it. This is entirely normal, and providing you don't let it influence you too much, it won't have much of an effect. However, in some extreme cases, a lack of self-confidence could have huge implications on your performance, and could ruin your ride before you have even turned a pedal.

The majority of amateur cyclists shy away from success, and lose some of their confidence based on a previous bad experience. Top cyclists however, use this as a driving force. In fact, much research has shown confidence as the most influential factor that distinguishes between successful and less successful athletes.

What is self-confidence?

Sport psychologists define self-confidence as the belief that you can successfully perform a desired behaviour. According to psychologist Albert Bandura, this is achieved through four primary sources:

Performance accomplishments

This is what we have achieved through training and competition. Repeated success leads to positive expectation and enhanced self-belief. If your training has gone well – which we hope it has – then you should be confident that you can complete your sportive. Remember earlier on we talked about the importance of setting attainable, but challenging goals? This is a great way to build confidence.

Vicarious experience

Also known as modelling. It is believed that athletes can gain confidence from viewing performances of others at a similar level to them. If you're apprehensive about your ride, find someone who has ridden that distance or event before and find out how they got on. Chances are, it won't be as bad as you think.

Verbal persuasion

We all like a pat on the back. Having people show confidence in your ability is hugely beneficial. It

strokes our egos and helps us feel better about ourselves. Riding with a friend will help, as you will be able to bounce off each other during your ride and give each other a high five once you have finished.

Emotional arousal

Thinking about your event can be enough to increase your heart rate and make the palms of your hands sweat. Look at these symptoms in a positive way rather than negatively. This is your body's natural preparation for performance. It's a good sign that you are reacting this way and shows that you are ready.

Remember: self-confidence is a good thing. In fact, it's a great thing and is a very useful tool to have. It could be the difference between getting through your sportive and racing through it.

Coach's perspective

Ex-pro and director of Forme coaching, Dan Fleeman believes mental preparation plays a huge role in cycling.

The mental side of sport is massively underrated. It's quite tricky to get people talking about it, because not many people would want to admit that their confidence is low or that they are struggling mentally.

If your confidence is low, straight away you're starting on the back foot. Take Mark Cavendish. Now he's got this huge mental belief that he is the best. Luckily, he has the ability to back it up. But if he didn't have that confidence he wouldn't perform anywhere near as well as he could.

Ability will take you the top, but without the confidence you will struggle. You need to believe you can perform well in events, and that you can beat your opponents or achieve a personal best.

You have to get the balance right though, as it's a fine line between confidence and cockiness. When I feel like I'm lacking confidence I always remind myself that the majority of us are all born with two arms and two legs. If one person can do it, then there's no reason why another person can't, providing they've put in the adequate effort and training.

When you're on the start line of your sportive, you've got to think that you've done the maximum training, the maximum preparation and done everything you could to get the best performance. There is no reason why you shouldn't go out and perform to the best of your ability. Remind yourself of the hard work you have done and you should have no fear of tackling the event.

ONE WEEK TO GO
CARBO-LOADING

Carbo-loading is about more than having a big bowl of pasta the night before a race. Done properly it can have a huge effect on your performance.

Fuel up

Your body normally only stores enough glycogen to fuel 90 minutes of exercise, often much less if you don't refuel properly after your training sessions. Carbo-loading crams carbohydrate into your glycogen stores till they become supercompensated, which can increase your endurance by as much as 20 per cent or improve your time by 2–3 per cent. In a 100-mile sportive you could finish as much as 15 minutes faster just by thinking carefully about your food intake in the days leading up to it.

Carbo-loading is only needed for significant competitive events of over 90 minutes. It isn't something you need to do every weekend before your long training ride but you do need to try it a few times before a key event to know how your body responds and what foods work for you. One thing to

watch out for is that glycogen is stored in your muscles along with water. If you've effectively super-compensated you will gain a little weight, in fact, full glycogen loading can increase your body weight by 2kg but it is only temporary and will go during the event.

Carbo-loading needs to go hand in hand with tapering for your event. While it is important to ride in those final few days to keep your legs feeling loose and ready, you need to ease off on the volume and intensity of your rides. Rides will be an hour or less at an easy pace just throwing in a few very short, very sharp sprints to keep yourself primed and fresh. As you gradually taper your exercise in the final three days, focus on eating a high-carb diet and aim to consume 8–12g of carbohydrate per kilogram of body weight. Make sure you eat straight after any riding and don't let yourself feel hungry at any point. If you need to you can start your carbo-loading phase a week before your event as your elevated muscle glycogen levels can be maintained for as much as five days. This could be helpful if you know you are going to struggle to manage your diet whilst travelling to an event.

Carbo-loading requires a vast amount of food. Ensuring that you are getting the 8–12g per kg of your body weight isn't as easy as it sounds. Often riders think they are eating enough because they

Tell-tale signs

- Ear infections
- Increased muscle pain
- Sore throats
- Coloured nasal discharged

Now you must stop riding and rest. Stay indoors and avoid exercising. Never ride with a fever. A fever is your body's defence mechanism against these types of infections. It encourages your metabolism to speed up, so your body starts to produce more antibodies in order to kill invading germs.

Getting back to it

The biggest problem we face once we have fallen victim to an infection is deciding when to start riding again. More often than not, we feel weak and unfortunately lose some of our fitness. Research has shown that athletes or regular trainers who haven't exercised for 10 days due to an illness have lost anything up to 10 per cent in endurance. It's no wonder people are itching to get back on the bike again before they are actually ready. You may not want to hear it, but be patient and take your time. Getting back on the bike too soon could cause your infection to come back. Make sure you are com-

pletely free of it before going back out on two wheels again. When you do go back out, ride within your limits. Your reactions won't be at their sharpest, nor your fitness, so take extra caution. Conserve your energy and stay warm. Acknowledge that you are going to be weaker and you won't be able to ride for as long as you are used to. Don't panic, this is normal, and in time, you will become stronger again.

Exercise to stay healthy

Exercising is a great natural way to protect you from picking up colds. During moderate bouts of exercise, immune cells circulate through the body much quicker, enabling them to kill bacteria and viruses that enter out body. Professor David Nieman of Appalachian State University stated that when moderate exercise is repeated on a near daily basis, there is a cumulative effect that leads to a long-term response.

Quick tip

For each day of fever, take it easy for two days. For examples, four days of fever would require eight days of rest/recovery.

Balancing act

Immunity is not just affected by vitamin and mineral status but a range of other factors too including the presence of tissue damage, inflammation, or the depletion of certain macronutrients during exercise.

For example, training on low-carbohydrate stores has been linked with an increase release of the stress hormone cortisol, an increase in the immune systems inflammatory response and a decrease in the production of protective immune markers. One of the benefits of consuming carbohydrate on the bike is that this assists in maintaining adequate carbohydrate stores to prevent this negative response.

Poor protein intake has also been found to negatively affect immune function too, with a landmark study by researcher Chandra in 1999 clearly illustrating an increased incidence of opportunistic infection.

so as to avoid wasted effort or risking pinch punctures, however, the last thing you want to be doing is tweaking cables, changing saddles or adjusting brakes. It can be tempting to start playing around with the components on your bike, 'just to make sure' but the reality is, you don't want to make any changes this late in the day. By this point you should be completely comfortable in your bike position, set up and trust that your brakes and gears are not going to cause you problems on the day. You've prepared your mind and body so you need to take any mechanical stresses out of the equation so as to fully focus on your performance.

ONE WEEK TO GO

PREPARING YOUR BIKE

We always recommend learning the basics about how your bike works, practising a speedy tyre change and always carrying at least two tubes for the eventuality of a flat.

The first thing is to leave yourself plenty of time so that you know your bike is good to go, which will eliminate the need to make last-minute adjustments. We recommend taking your bike to a shop for a service a week in advance. Find one that you trust by asking around locally or opting for a good chain. Double-check the time you can expect to pick it back up and make sure you've allowed for that in your final week schedule. By doing this, you'll be safe in the knowledge that it's signed off by a professional bike mechanic, plus you will also have time to take it for a spin in the time between the service and your event day, just to check you're 100 per cent happy with your well-oiled machine.

When it comes to the night before your big ride you'll need to make sure your tyres are fully inflated

Quick tip

In the weeks leading up the to event, learning the basics about how your bike works, practise a speedy tyre change and on the day itself carry at least two tubes for the eventuality of a flat.

ONE DAY
TO GO

ONE DAY TO GO

NIGHT-BEFORE NUTRITION

Your evening meal the day before your big event will play a part in fuelling the efforts of the next day's event so you need to be sure that it is high in carbohydrate to keep your muscle stores topped up. Choose a dish you enjoy and make sure you have a serving of good-quality protein and plenty of fruit and veg so it's not just a carb feast. It doesn't have to be a huge meal and neither does it have to be pasta. A small glass of wine or beer with your meal if you normally enjoy a drink isn't a bad thing either, it will help relax you.

Dos and dont's

- Avoid spicy foods. You don't want to still be tasting them the next day
- Don't eat anything new that may disagree with your stomach
- Drink plenty of water with your meal
- Add a little extra salt if the weather is hot. It will help the next day
- Don't eat too much fibrous food
- Eat early enough so that your meal doesn't interfere with getting a good night's sleep

Experts' perspectives

Lynne Coldray runs cycling B&B La Vélo Jaune based at the foot of Alpe d'Huez. She has competed in many sportives and helped her guests get the most from their Marmotte and Étape experiences.

Christopher Bland is host and owner of cycling holiday company Allons-y-Pyrenees. He has ridden many of the tough Pyrenean sportives as well as helping his guests prepare for the events they have come to ride. He lives within riding distance of the Tourmalet.

I don't think people worry about not having enough to eat as the day before an event seems to be a big eat! Our guests always request 'carbs' loads of pasta. We tend to cook a similar meal before any event, it is what we would have and seems to fit what the guests want: home-made soup with plenty of fresh baguette, pasta with Bolognese or vegetarian sauce and a green salad, fruit crumble and custard. There is always plenty of food; we do double portions. Guests don't tend to drink alcohol the night before but have lots of water. I always have a glass of red wine, I saw the French riders do it before the Étape so thought it couldn't be a bad thing.

Guests generally want to eat something high in carbs yet pretty plain and non-spicy or full of garlic. Lasagne is always pretty good or pasta bakes something like that and if I'm still hungry I fill up on French bread. Before the Étape, Keren [wife and co-owner] will go through the menu with guests in advance to check everyone's requirements. Porridge in the morning with honey or dried fruits before races or big rides in the mountains is often requested.

ONE DAY TO GO

ARE YOU PREPARED?

IS EVERYTHING READY?

The smallest things can have a big impact on your event day. If you're running around trying to find your drink bottles or kit you will significantly increase your stress levels and this can detract from things going smoothly.

Any factors you can control should be considered so that you remove any unnecessary anxiety and become entirely focused on resting and preparing for your big day.

With one day to go you obviously need to limit any running around so that you're legs are fresh and rested. That's why it's good to have a checklist so you can calmly sit down and tick everything off, safe in the knowledge you can get a good night's sleep and won't be rushing in the morning. Here's a run-down of what you need to do the day before:

- Having a *pre-race routine* helps many riders to focus. This may be the order in which you get up and have your breakfast or it could mean a ritual that allows you to calmly visualise how you want the day ahead to go. Whatever this routine may be, it's a good idea to allow yourself plenty of time to run through everything you need to, and get to the start line in time.
- *Plan your journey* well in advance and check transport links or traffic updates where possible to avoid hold ups.
- *Check out the weather forecast* and lay out all of your kit the night before, however if you are participating in a UK sportive it's probably best to have a lightweight rain shell in your clothing collection just in case! If you're travelling abroad, just make sure you have a thorough checklist as you pack.

Psychologically, good logistical preparation will complement all the hard work you've put in physically and give you the best possible chance of success on the day.

Fitter, Further, Faster Checklist
- ☐ Drink bottles
- ☐ Chosen energy drink
- ☐ Any energy foods you've chosen
- ☐ Clothing
- ☐ Cycling shoes
- ☐ Helmet
- ☐ Warm clothing for post event
- ☐ Bike/wheels
- ☐ Basic bike check – e.g. are your tyres pumped up/are your quick release levers secure?
- ☐ Race numbers/chip/ID depending on entry requirement

Expert's perspective

Lynne Coldray on preparing her guests for their event:

Fortunately nothing has gone wrong for us either racing or in sportives. We always make sure our bikes are in good working order so the day before is a check not a panic, clean, oiled, good tyres, inner tubes without patches, spares sorted. Always take the following: two inner tubes, two gas canisters, two canister adaptors, a spare bit of tyre to patch a hole in your, mini multi-tool, chain link. We always sort everything out the day before, clothes, event food, event drink. I am a bit anal and I even lay out my kit in the order I am going to put it on!

Athlete's perspective

Pete Mitchell rides for Great Britain and explains how he keeps calm before an event. You may find a different method, but reminding yourself that you've put the hard work in is important for your confidence at this stage.

Immediately before a big event the adrenalin and the nerves of the occasion mean that you're as up for it as you're ever going to be. To control anxiety I have visualisation cards for every effort I could do in competition and each tells me what I need to run through in my head. It just takes away all the stress because you remind yourself that you know what you're doing.

ONE DAY TO GO

RELAX!

After many months of hard work, you're finally here – it's the eve of your big day. Now is the time to rest and relax.

With less than 24 hours to go, there is nothing else you can do. You've got the miles in the legs, the plan laid out in your mind, and providing you've done a little research, you should know the route you are riding.

If your training hasn't gone to plan, don't stress about it. That won't help, in fact, it will make it worse. Worrying and panicking won't raise your fitness levels.

If your body is under a state of stress, you will struggle to sleep as well. While a lack of sleep won't ruin your day, it will make it everything seem a little harder. So do try and relax. Of course you are going to be a little nervous and excited. Months of planning, training and preparing have all been built up for this. It would be quite bizarre if you didn't feel these feelings. But try turning those thoughts around. Look at your nervousness and anxiety in a

positive way. That knot in your stomach isn't nerves at all. It's excitement.

Remind yourself why your rode your bike in the first place: for fun. Reiterate to yourself that bike riding is enjoyable, and that you love doing it. Tomorrow is your reward for all the hard work you have put in.

If you are feeling pent up, engross yourself in an activity that takes your mind off the event. Read a good book or perhaps watch a film. Why not stick your headphones in and put your feet up?

With just one day to go, the key is to relax as much as you can. Nerves are good as it shows that you are alert and aware of what is to come, but there is a fine line between nervousness and stress. Both of which are very different and have different influences on the body.

There's not much else we can say now, other than get off to bed early and get a decent night's sleep. Good luck!

ONE DAY TO GO
FAQ

I don't feel like eating. What should I do?

It's crucial to give your body what it needs in the final few days prior to your target event. Eating and drinking right is the key to getting the most out of your body and so you shouldn't be scrimping on calories and ending up on the start line at a deficit. It's not unheard of to lose your appetite when nerves start to hit so there are ways to cope with this. Carbohydrate drinks or nutrient-dense foods, such as malt loaf, sweets or even ice cream, can provide the carbohydrate and protein that you need and will slip down easily.

Will a few beers wreck my performance the next day?

Relaxing and having a glass of wine or one beer with your meal the night before your sportive is absolutely fine, however, having several could have a negative impact on your performance so is best avoided. Having too much alcohol the night before could leave you dehydrated and prevent you from feeling your best the following day. You've worked hard, so leave the drinking until the after-party. At this point,

you're better off sipping a sports nutrition drink than a double vodka!

What will happen if I don't have enough time to warm up?

If it's a long sportive you don't need to worry too much if, despite your best efforts, you arrive late and miss your warm-up. However, we'd always recommend some form of warm-up, so in this scenario bear in mind that you are starting the event cold. If this does happen, you will benefit from taking it fairly easy during the first few miles so you don't go into the red straight away. Going out guns blazing will impact on your performance later in the day.

ukcyclingevents.co.uk

Registrati

THE BIG
DAY

You could of course take your preferred food along with you, but you will only be able to take as much as your jersey pocket permits. So these final few hours at home are vital. Trust us: if you don't, you will be kicking yourself two thirds of the way around your sportive.

What do we need?

Just like when you were training, your body needs a mixture of proteins, fats and carbohydrates. Your body will be expending a lot of energy, breaking down a lot of muscles, and giving off a lot of heat. As we all know by now, we need to refuel with what we are losing.

Providing you ate correctly the night before, now should be a case of topping up your system. Don't fall into the trap that just because you ate well the night before you needn't today, because you do.

THE BIG DAY

THE BIG DAY
MORNING NUTRITION

By now you should have a fairly good understanding of nutrition and hydration, the importance of them as a pair, and how to implement and utilise both to aid training, performance and recovery.

The hours leading up to your event are no different and nutrition and hydration should be taken just as seriously. If ignored, you could run into some serious trouble out on the road.

This is your only chance where you have complete control to fill up your body with what you want and with what it so desperately needs. The moment you leave the comfort of your own home, you will be relying on sport supplements and whatever the petrol garage on the way has to offer.

Along the route of your sportive, there should be feed stations. But don't rely on them as they might have run out of certain things when you get to them, or perhaps stock food you're not fond of.

Five low GI foods good for morning

Food	GI
Porridge	42
Muesli	56
Oatmeal biscuit	55
Apple	38
Skim milk	32

Don't rush

Giving yourself time in the morning to eat isn't just to avoid a manic rush, but it's also to give your body a chance to digest and utilise whatever it is you are feeding it.

Many people will scoff and fill themselves up an hour before their event; some leave it until moments before. What they don't know is doing that can have a detrimental affect. Ingesting, digesting and storing carbohydrates within the liver can take anything up to four hours. Eating so close to your event will only lead to bloating, tiredness and even sickness. It's not rocket science that if you fill your stomach up to the brim and then go off to ride, you're not going to feel too great. You're giving your body too much to do and it can't deal with it.

So make sure you eat well in advance of your event. It's fine to top up with smaller items, such as a cereal bar, or sip of drink, but for anything else, you must give yourself time.

Don't forget about H$_2$O!

If we have eaten well the evening before, our bodies already have a base fuel. And while you can make sure you are fully hydrated before you go to bed, you will lose a lot of fluids by the time you wake up. That's why we need to take on as much fluid as we can, way before we ride, to give our bodies a chance to absorb it all. As Andy Blow said earlier, take on a 500ml electrolyte drink an hour and a half before your ride. By the time your ride comes along, you shouldn't have any fluid washing around in your stomach, as it should have either been soaked up, or urinated out.

Getting it wrong

We all get it wrong from time to time – nobody is perfect. I remember one of the first sportives I ever rode and I got it terribly wrong. The night before I ate a huge bowl of pasta and chicken and felt really good. However, I fell into the trap so many have fallen into. I completely ignored my breakfast. I didn't feel like I needed to eat in the morning as I had such a huge meal the night before. I grabbed one slice of toast, had a mouthful of tea and left for my sportive.

The next few hours can only be described as a living nightmare. I could barely turn the pedals; every slight incline felt like a mountain peak, and every gentle warm breeze felt like a gale force headwind.

I stopped at the first feed station and stuffed myself with as much food as I could. This proved even more disastrous as my body could not cope with the sheer abundance of food I was putting in it. I won't go into further details, but let's just say, that I will never make the mistake of not eating the morning of the ride ever again.

Robert Hicks (co-author)

Do it like the pros

Sarah Storey is a British road and track cyclist who has won multiple gold medals at the Paralympic Games as well as two British national track championships. This is her routine.

I eat porridge for breakfast with honey and blueberries. The porridge is great for sustained energy, the blueberries have antioxidant qualities and the honey is another good source of quick energy.

British track sprinter, Matt Crampton who is part of the Team Sky track programme says:

If my event is a little bit later in the day, I try to eat a second meal consisting of either a jacket potato with tuna, a hearty sandwich or a pasta meal. I would usually have some sort of energy bar or snack a lot closer to training.

gear and gradually build up your leg speed so you are pedalling fast and fluidly. Click through all your gears whilst using the inner ring to check they are working smoothly, then switch to the big ring and do the same. In a moderate gear maintain a steady pace till you are beginning to breathe regularly and deeply, around Zones 2 to 3. You may feel sluggish, slow or lacking in power during your warm-up but don't worry about this, it is nerves and will pass as soon as you get started.

Ease off the pace as you get back toward the start so your heart rate and breathing slows again. Often you have to wait at the start for some time so there is no point arriving there dripping in sweat and breathing deeply. Make sure that your bike is in the gear you want to start in before you line up. Even if you have to wait for a bit it is still worth warming up, the benefits will stay with you for a while and it will feel much better than starting from cold.

THE BIG DAY
WARM-UP

Warming up before an event serves several purposes. It is first and foremost about raising your body temperature, lifting your heart rate and preparing your body for exercise as explained on pages 44–45. It also allows you to check your bike is in good working order, which is particularly important if you have travelled with it, and is a good opportunity to get your mind ready and focused on the task ahead.

How to warm up
The longer the event the shorter the warm-up needs to be. Track sprinters who are only racing for a handful of seconds will spend up to an hour gradually warming up and working on their leg speed using the rollers in the track centre. For sportive riders who are going to be in the saddle for several hours you only really need 10–20 minutes to check your bike and get brain and body prepared for the start.

The easiest way to warm up at a large event is to do a short road ride near to the start area. Keep an eye on the time and ride five minutes away from the start and then five minutes back. Start off in your easiest

Warm-up music

Music has been shown to have a very strong effect on sporting performance. While you shouldn't use headphones during an event for safety reasons, having your favourite tunes on while you warm up can be a very useful way of helping you to get into the right frame of mind to perform well. The right music for you can help psych you up, ready to ride.

Music is incredibly personal so there is no point in us making recommendations but generally tracks with a fast tempo, 90–120 beats per minute, seem to be more arousing and uplifting, perfect for a warm-up. Put together a playlist of songs that make you feel good, gives you a lift and energises you, which you can play on the way to the event and during your warm-up ride. If you do a lot of events it is a good idea to save your playlist for event days only so that you don't get too familiar with the music as it may begin to lose its effect. That way it is always associated with warming up and the excitement of being at an event.

Things to do while you warm up

- Check your gears
- Check your brakes
- Listen to your bike so you know nothing is rubbing
- Play uplifting music
- Mentally rehearse your pacing plan
- Go through the course in your mind
- Remind yourself of all the successful training you have done
- Focus on positive feelings of excitement to get started

THE BIG DAY
ON THE LINE
WHAT TO EXPECT?

Once you get to the start line of your event there is nothing more you can do except trust your preparation and get ready to give it everything you've got.

Allow yourself plenty of time in the morning for finding your way around the start area and getting ready in a calm, unrushed manner. There are normally two key priorities: collecting your number and identifying where the toilets are! Sign-on desks close well before the start so unless your toilet needs are desperate, or the queue very short, collect your number first. Find out where and how the numbers need to be displayed – you don't want your efforts to be wasted because your finishing time couldn't be recorded.

Having a routine is a really good way of managing pre-event nerves. If you do the same things in the same order every time you are less likely to forget anything. Get your bike ready first: check tyre pressures, put race numbers on, check wheels are in correctly and go through the gears just to be sure nothing has been knocked about on the bike rack or in the car.

The next step is to get into your own kit; this is when you can start to focus on your body. Take care pulling up your socks and putting your shoes on, look at your legs and remember how much training and hard work they have done. Give them a light massage as you rub in your sun cream or embrocation. Make sure you get another toilet stop in, it's normal to need to go as many as three or four times even once you are at the start. Keep drinking either water with electrolytes or an energy drink up to 60 minutes before the start.

Do your warm-up as discussed on pages 173–174. At big sportive events, where you are required to be in your holding pen for sometime before the start, you may not be able to warm up on your bike. In this case make your way to your pen in good time, but not too early, there is no point in hanging around getting cold for any longer than you need to. If you know you are going to be waiting for a long time, take a jersey or jacket that you can hand to a friend, or supporter. If that is not possible a bin bag or newspaper under your jersey will keep the chill off and you can hand this to a marshal to throw away shortly before the start.

Positioning on the start line

When choosing your place on the start line be realistic about your abilities and your goals. If you are confidently fit and determined to be in the mix from the start aim to be near, but not necessarily on, the front row. If you aren't planning a fast start you may feel more comfortable toward the middle or back where there is a bit more space. Wherever you are stood you can guarantee that the people around you are also feeling nervous and trying to concentrate on their race plan. Everyone deals with nerves in different ways, some people go quiet but others like to talk themselves up. Try not to get caught up in any banter or any discussion of how much training or preparation you've done. It can exacerbate your feelings of nerves and you don't know how fast, or slow, the people around you are.

Getting started

As soon as the gun goes or barriers are lifted all nerves evaporate and it is finally time for your legs to do exactly what you have been training them for. The first 15–20 minutes of any event is always a little bit hectic, particularly road races or mass start sportives. Riders will be jostling for position and looking for a good wheel to follow.

How you handle the initial part of a ride very much depends on your overall goals. If you are aiming to do well in a race, or get a fast finishing time, it is imperative that you move to a position that is near but not on the front. This should get you into a fast

moving group and keep you away from any crashes. It may mean that you have to stretch yourself a little bit to make the group but that will ultimately help you get a better result, so be prepared to suffer for the first few miles. However, if your aim is simply to finish or you are looking for a good finishing time but not to race, it is better to settle into the sustainable pace you have decided on. Overreaching your abilities by getting sucked into a fast group can have huge repercussions later on in the event. Stay calm and focused on your own pacing strategy. Be aware of your body, your effort level and the decisions you are making.

Kit bag extras

- Safety pins
- Cable ties
- Toilet roll
- Newspaper or carrier bags

Athlete's perspective

Endurance specialist Mike Cotty shares his experiences on the start line.

Despite riding competitively for over 20 years, the start sensations for me are always the same. The adrenalin builds and it feels like someone has tied a knot in my stomach. There's always a certain amount of fanfare that surrounds the start. I try and relax, focus, and quietly visualise the ride ahead. I now embrace my nervous energy like a friend and use it as a positive to get the best performance from myself. I know without it, something just wouldn't be right.

Quick tip

Nerves are good, it shows that you care about the event you are about to do and that your body is primed for it. Nerves disappear as soon as you start so don't let them overwhelm you.

Experts' perspectives

Lynne Coldray has participated in many events, and helps other people get the most out of their sportives. This is what runs through her mind right before the start.

Being on the start line is very emotional, I always have tears behind my sunglasses, total mixed emotion: excitement at doing something I have trained for and want to do and apprehension – how will I do? Even if it's not a race, it is, everyone wants to do their best. The 'event' feel always gets to me, the smell of coffee at French events, the noise initially of everyone chatting then the nearer the start times the quieter people are. There is often music, there are certain tunes that always bring back sportive memories. Every time I am on a start line I ask myself 'why', and at the same time know I love it. It's good to know exactly what is coming up. I always want to see the event profile, so as I go I know what's to come – the Marmotte I see as four hills (big ones) then I tick them off as I go.

Christopher Bland on getting ready to race:

Being on the start line is exciting, I always get butterflies. It is great to take in the atmosphere of so many riders getting ready for a race and see what everyone does to prepare and it is a chance to chat and meet new people. I always have a plan in my head of how I am going to tackle the course ... not that it always pans out that way!

and other road debris as well as other riders, putting yourself and others in danger.

THE BIG DAY
STAY FOCUSED

You're well into your ride now, piercing through the wind, swallowing up the miles of tarmac that lies in front of you. Your heart is beating through your chest, your senses are on edge, and you just want to go harder and harder.

While we don't want to put a stop to your fun, we don't want you to go too hard at first. It's important you stay focused. This can be hard, as your mind is ticking over at a million miles per hour, but you have got to try and control it. If you're not fully concentrating, your attention narrows and you may not be aware of what you're doing or your surroundings. We call this tunnel vision.

Many people at the beginning of a sportive are so excited, they fly off as fast as they can, ignore their hydration and nutrition needs, and then wonder why they come to a virtual standstill 5 or 6 miles later. Also, by not taking in your surroundings, you may be unaware of road conditions such as turns, potholes

Keep your concentration

Follow these three simple points, which will help you remain focused and remind you of what you need to be doing.

1. Breathing
Deep, controlled breathing helps lower your heart rate and reduces stress levels, as well as alleviate tension throughout your body. By consciously taking deep breaths, you are working your mind, and avoiding the chances of it wondering off on a tangent. Slowing everything down gives everything a more controlled feel. A relaxed body is far more efficient than a tense one.

2. Self-talk
Although it may seem a little odd, talking to yourself on the bike is one of the key components in sports psychology to help keep concentration levels. Speak to yourself in the second person. Tell yourself to think, to focus, and to calm down. Say it out loud. Repeat it to yourself over and over again. You could even use this technique to prepare yourself for the big climb, or technical descent.

3. Chunking
A sportive of any real length is going to require a fair few hours in the saddle. It's extremely difficult to concentrate for such long periods of time. Try breaking down your route into sections with appropriate changes in focus of attention at various points. This will keep you mind fresh and fully focused on each section.

Quick tip

It helps to have practised fixing a puncture or rejoining a chain a few times before your event. Get someone to time you so you feel under pressure.

THE BIG DAY

WHEN THINGS GO WRONG

However well prepared you are for an event occasionally things do go wrong, some are within your control, some are not. Staying calm and thinking clearly will get you back on track quickly. If things do go wrong, how you cope with the upset to your game plan can either minimise or exacerbate your time loss.

Troubleshooting
You have a puncture

Don't mess around riding on a flat, stop as soon as you safely can. If you are in a group shout puncture and raise your hand. Gradually drift to the side of the road so riders can move round you without causing an accident. Stay calm as rushing may cause you to pinch the new tube or overlook a sharp object in the tyre. Done smoothly you shouldn't lose more than two to three minutes. When you get back on your bike get back up to speed as quickly as you can but don't be tempted to push yourself into the red trying to make up lost time as this can create its own problems.

You haven't been eating and drinking

As soon as you realise you are behind on your fuelling plan try and catch up by having a gel and swigging back plenty of fluids. Avoid the high-fat, high-sugar cakes, biscuits or snacks at a feed station as this will slow down the absorption of the energy you desperately need and may result in stomach discomfort.

You 've got stomach problems

Hot weather can play havoc with your digestion if you are not used to it. Try to get down as much plain water or isotonic energy drink as you can. You may not fancy them much but gels leave your stomach quicker than bars, so you may find avoiding solid food helps.

You started too hard and now you are paying for it

Make sure you are fuelling properly as your earlier efforts will have taken a lot of energy. Fix a comfortably steady pace and simply keep going. Keep a smooth high cadence and focus on steady breathing and strong pedalling. In a long event you will often go through good and patches.

You crash

Check your body first and bike second. Head injuries, deep cuts and broken bones obviously require medical attention so don't try to be a hero. However plenty of people have finished events with gravel rash and bruising so if your injuries are superficial you may be able to carry on, if you feel able to.

Check your bike is undamaged and safe to ride. Before you get back on it spin the wheels in the frame to check they aren't buckled, go through the gears and particularly check the rear mech and drop out is unbent, check your brakes. If neither you nor your bike are in a bad way then get going.

Expert's perspective

Christopher Bland on preparation – and getting it wrong:

Make sure you have checked out the course of your sportive, especially when there are several different length courses in one event. We had one guest who took a wrong turning and ended up missing a col out nearly finishing the race in the medals. Luckily he was so chuffed to get to a fully stocked-up feed station ahead of the field that he got carried away refuelling so the leaders actually caught him up. It could have been very embarrassing for all and difficult to explain in another language!

THE
FINISH
LINE

THE FINISH LINE
WARM-DOWN

Once your wheels have crossed the finish line, you'll be overcome with a whole array of emotions. Some riders are relieved, others express joy, and many cry. Everybody has different ways of expressing emotion and finding the valve to release the huge pressure that has resided in your body for however many months.

For some it may seem like this moment would never come, while others are left somewhat deflated as now it's all over. It is these mixed thoughts and emotions that lead to people ignoring their bodily needs slowing down their recovery and risking sickness a few days after your event.

Although the riding has finally stopped, your body hasn't, and is still trying to cope with the stress you have been putting it under for the past few hours. Your muscles still require oxygen, and your heart will continue to beat fast in order to get the oxygenated blood to the vital parts of the body. Your respiratory rate is also high, as are the levels of adrenalin and lactic acid in the muscles.

You may feel that your body is craving for a sit down in the sun with a beer in your hand, but there is one thing you must do before that, which it needs much, much more – and that is an efficient warm-down.

You what?
Throughout this book we have spoken about the importance of an efficient warm-up, and the effects it has on the body. A warm-down is no exception.

Ex-GB Olympic medallist and road racer, Rob Hayles reiterates this: 'Warm downs are so often overlooked. I'm a huge advocator of a warm-down. It helps your body recover much quicker and gets the pain out of your legs.'

Like warm-ups, the benefits to some are still somewhat vague, with many believing that it's a waste of time, and does nothing else apart from tire you out even more. How can riding your bike for an extra 15 minutes after you've completed a five-hour ride help the body? It seems a reasonable question to ask, but the fact of the matter is, an efficient warm-down has a number of benefits that not only immediately help the body cope with the demands of exercise, but reduce the draining feelings one encounters hours and days after your ride.

How to warm down
The great thing about a warm-down is that they don't take very long. Just spend 10 to 15 minutes

riding your bike, gradually bringing the pace down. If you're not fussed on the time you set for your sportive, take the last ten minutes to do this, coupled with long deep breaths. Alternatively, you can ride around the car park or along another stretch of road after your sportive in order to achieve this. Remember: the idea is to gradually bring yourself down from the dizzying heights you were hitting when you were riding. It may not seem like much, but it will make a huge difference.

Warm-down benefits

Stopping abruptly can cause blood to pool around your muscles, which results in insufficient blood flow and oxygen to the brain causing light headedness, dizziness and even fainting.

A correct warm-down will:

- Aid in the removal of waste products – most notably lactic acid
- Lower the level of adrenalin in the blood and therefore reducing stress
- Reduce the impact of DOMS
- Help the heart rate return to its resting state

Expert's perspective

Matt Rabin, Garmin Team Barracuda, shares his views on warm downs:

The most important thing as I see it, that is so overlooked by normal cyclists and even professionals is to warm down. After cycling you need to bring your body temperature back down steadily to its original state. Your sympathetic nervous system is in overload, firing up, buzzing, and now you've stopped. You've finished your ride, you've gone away, got showered and off you go. But your body is still firing. You've got to wind it down slowly. You've got to transition that period from full gas exercise and riding hard, into slowing down and into recovery mode. Your core body temperature starts to come down, your heart rate lowers, your muscles start to relax and it helps clear lactic acid. That warm-down period to me is the most important period. It's massive.

The duration of your warm-down all depends on the duration of your bike ride. For example, if your ride is for an hour, spend five to seven minutes cooling down. Finish your ride that little bit further away from your destination and spend the final leg cruising in. Nice and easy.

It's very interesting because it's only now that teams in the peleton are starting to adopt this approach and understand the importance of warm-downs.

It really helps to get your parasympathetic nervous system working, calms you down, and helps make the transition from exercise to rest to recovery. That's my number one, golden tip.

Quick tip

Don't forget to eat! As we have stressed throughout the book, recovery is so important. Take the time to feed your body, whether it's a recovery drink or some chicken and chips from the local pub!

'My favourite has got to be the Chiltern 100 for me ... It's on my doorstep, hilly and picturesque.'

Andy Trisconi

'My first sportive was the Tour de France stage from London to Canterbury. I was equal parts hungry, emotional and exhausted due to the utter lack of pacing.'

Mike Smith

'I did the Étape du Tour Acte one last year and the feeling I had at the top of Alpe d'Huez was "that was *awesome*!"'

Ross James

'The time didn't matter, completing it was awesome and just made me want to do longer distances!'

Dave Brookes

'I was happy to have completed the challenge I set myself and thankful for the organiser to have put the event on!'

Jean-Sebastien Vecten

THE FINISH LINE

REAL RIDER STORIES

Finishing your first sportive is a fantastic achievement. We hear from riders about how they felt when they crossed the finish line for the first time, what their favourite event to date has been and how cycling dramatically changed one rider's life.

'My favourite sportive is the Haute Route as it doesn't get any tougher than that!'

Mark Turner

'I was fortunate enough to do the Cape Argus last year. I had some time out there, got a training programme together and flew up Chapman's peak, in fact I wished the ride was longer. The value of a few months' training for a target was very worthwhile and the sun was shining at the time.'

David O'Keeffe

'Flanders is my favourite sportive. I need more pave in my life!'

James Wakelin

Rider's perspective

Mary Estall has lost seven stone and explains how starting cycling and slimming down has changed her life.

"*I decided to lose weight because I couldn't live the lifestyle that I wanted to lead. While at uni in Bath I started going to the gym and my parents bought up my old bike that I had bought when I was about 12 and I literally couldn't cycle a mile. After finishing my degree I moved to London and started Weight Watchers. I realised that I could get around London quicker on a bike so parents lent me money to buy a hybrid.*

I took up cycling more seriously once I had lost the weight and it gave keeping the weight off a purpose. I joined Kingston Wheelers and really love the variety of people that cycle.

Cycling has taught me a lot. I have learnt that you can ride for a day and a half on a broken collarbone and also that front wheels and ducks don't mix.

Cycling makes me feel alive, you can watch the Tour de France from the comfort of your sofa or you can get out and feel a fraction of what the pros go through by cycling the same mountains.

Three years ago I had one hybrid but now I own a mountain bike and a road bike. I love seeing where my limits actually are and not where I think that they are. I have been track cycling, mountain biking in Morocco, and cycling in Majorca.

allowed that to be overshadowed by a very strong set of riders on the day. For this reason it's good to assess your own achievement based on your personal time, speed and how you felt at the end of it in order to move forward.

THE FINISH LINE

SELF-ASSESSMENT

HOW DID IT GO?

When you've finished your target event you may want to remember it forever and display your number on the mantle piece or perhaps try to bury your feelings and forget how hard it was. Either way, the evaluation process is useful as it allows you to look at all the positives and negatives in order to gain feedback for your next sportive.

Neuro-Linguistic Programming (NLP) is a technique many elite riders are using as a tool for personal development. NLP is an approach that can increase confidence, change unwanted behaviours and look at situations from different perspectives. This allows many athletes to understand and address aspects of their performances that they'd like to change. It's important to look at how well you did individually, for example, if you came near the back of the field it by no means indicates a failure, in fact, you may have achieved a personal best performance yet

Coach's perspective

NLP Coach Practitioner Avril Charlton explains how you can evaluate your performance using the NLP technique.

"The period of time following an event is a good opportunity to review your performance with respect to the goals you set for yourself beforehand.

So, refer back to the goals you set at the beginning of the book. If you fulfilled all of these, you can celebrate and congratulate yourself but also notice what you are thinking and saying about your success. Are you telling yourself it was your lucky day? Or that you deserved to do well because you trained hard? If you explain your success by telling yourself it was because the other competitors performed badly, then that will be very difficult to repeat. But if you can attribute your success to your personal, internal qualities then you can work out how to do more of what worked and achieve an even better result next time.

Our internal dialogue has a powerful effect on how we behave and reflects how we see ourselves. If you notice that you're telling yourself you 'never finish a ride with the group' or you 'always give up', you can challenge those thoughts by remembering a time when you did finish – and if this was your first sportive, find an example of another challenge in your life that you did complete.

NLP uses an approach called 'reframing'. It's based on the thinking that if you change the way you perceive an event then you can change its meaning for you. For example, if an event doesn't go how you wanted it to, instead of seeing the whole thing as a failure, look for what did go well. Change your focus to the successes, however small they might seem, and the more you look for them the more you will find. Instead of using the language and behaviour associated with failure, reframe your experience as a good opportunity to learn. Now you can begin to make changes in preparation for your next event.

We can be our own harshest critics but negative self-talk can damage self-belief and confidence. Changing the language you use can lead to a more positive outlook – you might find you begin to expect success and it becomes a self-fulfilling prophecy. Challenging your own beliefs and thoughts might seem strange at first but habits are formed through practice until they become automatic. So you can make reframing and positive thinking your new habit and become your own strongest supporter.

THE FINISH LINE

LOOK TO THE FUTURE, START AGAIN

We're pretty sure that once you've ridden your first sportive you'll soon be filling in your next entry form. Whether this is the start of your journey or you've just completed one of the many events in your calendar, now is a crucial time to look at the bigger picture.

While now is the moment to enjoy your achievement, eat that slice of cake, enjoy drinks with friends or throw a party, it's also time to look forward to the next target. Having a rest is crucial and eating and sleeping right in the following week is key to allowing your body to really benefit from the effort it has been through. If you come out of the event having given it everything, you'll feel like a good old rest afterwards and it may be worth booking that Monday off work! Hammering yourself in subsequent training sessions too soon may leave you feeling exhausted so you must bear in mind what your body has achieved and acknowledge you may feel tired after your peak. That said, when you reach your goal and everything has gone to plan it can, for some riders, leave you with a feeling of deflation because you've become so used to going out with a purpose, day after day. That's why it's a careful balance and during that rest period it can be helpful to plan your next target.

With every big training session or event it's always good to look forward, rather than thinking, 'phew that's over' and taking a month off. A little break is good but it doesn't mean you should ditch the bike all together or stop eating well, as it will become that much harder to get yourself back into a healthy routine again when you decide to resume training.

What next?

Having done your evaluation process it's time to reassess your goals and decide what's next. Do you want to push for a bigger distance? Or perhaps target the same event next year but beat your personal best? Whatever you decide, it's time to celebrate everything that went right and look at working on any weak points to go in even stronger for your next sportive.

You have now achieved something great, you've come a long way and it's important to recognise that. As you return to the goal-setting chapter, you'll be better equipped to train for that next event, and you'll have learnt a lot about yourself and your riding along the way. Good luck for the next sportive and beyond – we know you will achieve great things!

Athlete's perspective

UK track rider Dave Daniell explains why it's so important to give yourself the time to rest, relax and build enthusiasm for that next event after you've peaked for something so important to you.

"What I tend to do after competitions is have a little break, have time off and just forget about cycling for a bit because I think if you get straight back into training you do have that slump and your motivation is on the floor because there's a big high for the competition and then you have a big low. Normally what happens is you peak for these competitions so you're not going very well afterwards and everything tends to go against you. Therefore it's best just to put your feet up and enjoy life for a couple of weeks and then come back in being hungry again for the next competition.

INDEX

accidents, 94–95
aches, 60–61, 115
    see also pain
alcohol consumption, 136–137, 162, 163, 167
Allen keys, 25
anxiety, 144, 165
appetite, 117
Armstrong, Lance, 92
Armstrong Urine Colour Chart, 81–82

balance, 63
Bandura, Albert, 153
base layer, 23
big-gear starts, 104
bike fitting, importance of, 18–20, 54, 72
bike posture, 17
bike preparation, 159
biomechanics, 73
Bland, Christopher, 163, 177, 180
Blow, Andy, 81
Body Mass Index (BMI), 138
body measurements, 31
braking, 49, 52–53, 100
breathing, 178
Brookes, Dave, 185
burnout, 114–116
    aches, 115
    decrease in performance, 115
    fatigue, 116
    illness, 115
    mood swings, 115
    sleep, 115

cables, 29
cadence drills, 43, 104, 124
Cattermole, Jason, 57
Cavell, Phil, 20
Cavendish, Mark, 153, 154
chains, 28
chamois cream, 25
Charlton, Avril, 188
chiropractors, 74
chunking, 178
cleats, 21, 22
clothing, 22–24, 58, 121, 148
cold baths, 151
Coldray, Lynne, 163, 165, 177
colds, 115, 149, 157–158
collarbone breaks, 92, 93
cornering skills, 48–49, 96–97
Cotty, Mike, 142, 176
Crampton, Matt, 172
crashes, 94–95, 180
Crebbin, Michael, 73
Cundy, Jody, 113

Daniell, Dave, 190
data, 26, 27
dehydration
see hydration
delayed onset muscle soreness (DOMS), 60–61,
    183
Dickins, Anne, 63, 64

diet
    see nutrition
'Does Overtraining Exist?' (article), 114
Dowsett, Alex, 27
drafting, 46–47

electrolytes, 80, 81, 89, 90, 171
Estall, Mary, 186
etiquette rules, 47
event day
    breathing, 178
    checking the course, 180
    chunking, 178
    crashes, 180
    early race positioning, 176
    nerves, 176–177
    nutrition, 170–172, 179
    pre-start line preparation, 175
    punctures, 179
    self-talk, 178
    start line, 175–176
    starting too hard, 180
    staying focussed, 178
    stomach problems, 180
    warming up, 173–174, 175
    see also finish line
event distance, 120
event information, 146
event preparation
    bike preparation, 159
    day before event, 164–165
    night before event nutrition, 162–163
    relaxation, 166
    warming up, 167
excess body fat, 99
exercises, 62–63
    clams, 64–65
    modified bridge, 68
    side plank, 69
    squats, 65–66
    Superman series, 66–67
    weights, 62
eye problems, 92

Facebook, 58
fatigue, 116
feed stations, 140, 170
Fenner, Mike, 134
field testing, 31, 58
finish line
    riders' experiences, 185–186
    warm-down, 182–184
first aid, 92–93, 95
fitness development, 38–44, 102–109
    on the bike strength, 105
    building fitness, 39, 42–43
    cadence drills, 43, 104, 124
    consistency, 108
    lifestyle audit, 38
    long rides, 42, 102, 106, 122, 123, 126–127
    peaking early, 144
    power drills, 104, 105
    progress management, 39

quick-fire fitness, 122–125
threshold work, 104, 105
training menu, 102, 106–107
training zones, 41–43
weaknesses, 108
whilst at work, 130–131
    see also exercises; rest and recovery;
    warming up
Fleeman, Dan, 14, 154
foam rollers, 151
Food Guide Pyramid, 32–33
food supplements, 83–85
    caffeine, 86, 89
    energy bars, 86, 89
    fish oils, 87
    gels, 86, 88–89, 117
    Glucosamine, 87
    multivitamins and minerals, 86
    probiotics, 87
    protein supplements, 86–87
    recovery drinks, 87, 89–91
    sports drinks, 86
    vitamin C, 87
    zero-calorie drinks, 89
    see also nutrition
fractures, 93

gadgets, 26–27
gas inflators, 25
Gaywood, Simon, 151
gear changing, 28–29, 51, 104
gilets, 24
glasses, 23
gloves, 23, 24
Glycaemic Index (GI), 76–77
goal-setting, 12–17, 54
    long-term goals, 12
    reassessment, 189
    short-term goals, 12
    SMART method, 12–14
    sticking to goals, 14
gravel rash, 95
group riding
    see riding in a group

Halson, S.L., 114
Hayles, Rob, 45, 182
head injuries, 92–93
health checks, 16–17, 54
healthy eating
    see nutrition
heart problems, 17
heart rate monitoring, 26, 30, 141
helmets, 23, 92
Hersborg, Torben, 75
Hicks, Robert, 172
hills
    climbing, 50–51, 54, 98–99, 117, 123, 124,
        125
    descending, 52–53, 100–101, 104
Hincapie, George, 92
hydration, 80–81, 147, 171, 180
hypernatremia, 81

illness, 16–17, 115, 149
colds, 157–158
immune system, 157, 158
infections, 158
injuries, 16, 70–71
    bike fitting, 21
    first aid, 92–93, 95
International Journal of Sports Medicine, 132

jackets, 24
James, Ross, 185
jerseys, 23
Jeukendrup, A.E., 114

knee and arm warmers, 24

Lawson, Tim, 88–91, 136–137, 147
Le Grys, Dave, 58, 147
leg shaving, 151
lifestyle audit, 38
Lloyd, Dan, 100–101
long rides, 42, 102, 106, 122, 123, 126–127
Look (pedal system), 21

MacLean, Craig, 111
massage, 149, 150, 151
McCallum, James, 97, 137
mesocycles, 125
Millard, James, 28, 94
Mitchell, Pete, 120, 165
mood swings, 115
motivation, 58, 190
muscles
    cold baths, 150
    cores, 63
    delayed onset muscle soreness (DOMS),
        60–61, 182
    effects of tapering, 133–134
    foam rollers, 151
    massage, 150, 151
    pain, 72
    see also exercises; warm-down; warming up
music, 174

Neuro-Linguistic Programming (NLP), 187–188
Nieman, David, 158
nutrition, 32–37, 76–79, 120–121, 126–129, 147
    antioxidants, 78
    appetite, 117
    breakfast, 126–127
    carbo-loading, 155–156
    carbohydrates, 76–77, 89, 111–112, 127, 134,
        136, 158
    diet changes, 149
    energy balance, 76–77
    event day, 170–172
    Food Guide Pyramid, 32–33
    food shopping, 34, 36
    Glycaemic Index (GI), 76–77
    glycogen, 126, 127, 155–156
    night before event, 162–163, 167
    portion sizes, 37

protein, 77–78, 112
    for recovery, 111–112, 128
    weight maintenance, 136–139
    see also food supplements

O'Keeffe, David, 185
osteopathy, 75

pacing, 140–142
    effort levels, 140–141
    planning, 140
pain, 70–75
    awareness of, 72
    chiropractors, 74
    osteopathy, 75
    physiotherapy, 73
    relief of, 71
    types of, 70
    see also aches
Palfreeman, Roger, 72, 116
pedalling, 104, 107–108
pedals, 21, 72
performance measurement, 26–27
physiotherapy, 73
power drills, 104
power measurement, 26, 27, 141
Przybylski, Rachel, 131
psychological skills, 152–154
pumps, 25
punctures, 179

Rabin, Matt, 74, 183
Ranchordas, Mayur, 84–85
relaxation, 166
rest and recovery, 27, 39, 105, 108, 110–113
    nutrition for recovery, 111–112
    post event, 189–190
    process of, 110–111
    see also warm-down
resting heart rate, 30
riding in a group, 47, 48, 131, 142, 147
rollers, 25
Rowsell, Joanna, 90

saddles, 148
    height, 72
    injuries, 25, 72
    shape, 72
    tilt, 72
schedules, 12
Scripps, John, 31, 51, 53, 56
self-assessment, 30–31, 56–59, 120–121,
        146–147, 187–188
self-confidence, 58, 152–154
self-talk, 178
Shimano (pedal system), 21
shoes, 21, 22, 23
shorts, 22–23
sitting in
    see drafting
skills development, 121
    basics, 46–47, 57–58

climbing hills, 50–51, 54, 98–99, 117, 123,
        124, 125
    cornering skills, 48–49, 96–97
    descending hills, 52–53, 100–101, 107–108
    psychological skills, 152–154
sleep, 115, 144, 149, 150
slipstreaming
    see drafting
SMART goal-setting method, 12–14
Smith, Mike, 185
social networking, 58
socks, 22
spares, 25
speed measurement, 26
Speedplay (pedal system), 21
sports bras, 23
Sports Medicine, 114
SRM PowerControl 7, 27
static trainers, 25, 124
stings, 92
Storey, Sarah, 172
stress
    see burnout

tapering, 132–135, 155
technical nutrition, 88–91, 136
tights, 23–24
Tilt, Laura, 36, 156
time management, 56, 130–131
tools, 25
torque wrenches, 25
torx keys, 25
track pumps, 25
training
    listening to the body, 27
    mesocycles, 125
    overtraining, 114–116, 148
    pacing, 140–142
    static trainers, 25, 124
    tapering, 132–135, 155
    training menu, 102, 106–107
    zones, 41–43
    see also burnout; fitness development; rest
        and recovery
training peaks software, 27
tubes, 25
turbo trainers, 25, 124
Turner, Mark, 185
tyre levers, 25

Vecten, Jean-Sebastien, 185

Wakelin, James, 185
warm-down, 182–184
warming up, 44–45, 167, 173–174, 175
weight, 31, 56, 120, 136–139, 186
Wiggins, Bradley, 92
Williams, Huw, 17, 106, 125
winter clothing, 23–24
worry, 144, 165
Wyle-Smith, Roy, 92, 93